THE
ITALIAN
KITCHEN

THE
ITALIAN
KITCHEN

TRADITIONAL AND
CONTEMPORARY RECIPES
FOR PERFECT ITALIAN
CUISINE

First published in 2011

LOVE FOOD is an imprint of Parragon Books Ltd

Parragon
Queen Street House
4 Queen Street
Bath BA1 1HE, UK

ISBN: 978-1-4454-4453-6

Printed in China

Authors: Ingebrog Pils, Stefan Pallmer
Introduction: Linda Doeser
Photography: Martin Kurtenbach, Buenavista Studio
Cover images: Making Home Made Tomato Soup © Chris Cole/Getty Images ; Ingredients for Spaghetti
Squash Casserole © Jdomrose Photography Julia Duffy Domrose/Getty Images

This book uses imperial, metric, and US cup measurements. Follow the same units of measurement
throughout; do not mix imperial and metric. All spoon measurements are level: teaspoons are assumed
to be 5 ml, and tablespoons are assumed to be 15 ml. Unless otherwise stated, milk is assumed to be
whole, eggs and individual vegetables, such as potatoes, are medium, and pepper is freshly ground
black pepper.

The times given are an approximate guide only. Preparation times differ according to the techniques
used by different people and the cooking times may also vary from those given as a result of the type
of oven used. Optional ingredients, variations, or serving suggestions have not been included in the
calculations.

Recipes using raw or very lightly cooked eggs should be avoided by infants, the elderly, pregnant women,
convalescents, and anyone with a chronic condition. Pregnant and breast-feeding women are advised
to avoid eating peanuts and peanut products. People with nut allergies should be aware that some of
the prepared ingredients used in the recipes in this book may contain nuts. Always check the package
before use.

CONTENTS

INTRODUCTION

Italian food has conquered the world and there are few major cities that cannot boast a first class Italian restaurant. This unique cuisine delights with its fresh flavors, perfect combinations of ingredients, appetizing and often colorful appearance, and its reputation for being one of the healthiest diets in the world.

A brief history of Italian cuisine

The story of Italian cooking is inextricably linked to the story of the country itself. Besides constructing roads, piping fresh water across the country, and creating one of the greatest empires ever known, ancient Romans can also be credited with developing the first truly European cuisine. They were knowledgeable about food and farming and quick to exploit the natural riches of Italy—fish and shellfish from the Mediterranean and Adriatic, game from the hillsides, fresh fruit and vegetables transported daily from the countryside to the city. Farms raised goats, poultry, and lamb, and the Romans were expert in the art of curing meat, particularly pork to produce superb ham.

When the Roman Empire collapsed, barbarian invasions in the north of Italy destroyed much of its culture, including the cuisine. Conversely, the Saracen invasion in the south, especially in Sicily, brought new influences and new ingredients, such as rice, spinach, and almonds. They may even have been responsible for the invention of spaghetti. Later, as Europe settled down, the Renaissance, which was a period of new economic, political, cultural, and academic development, started to flourish and with it a revival of the art of cooking. The aristocratic families of Naples, Florence, and Milan delighted in good food and lavish banquets featuring soups, meat, game, poultry, fish, shellfish, vegetables, elaborate pies and tarts, a wide range of cheeses, and all kinds of fruit. A thriving spice trade brought new flavors for chefs to experiment with.

Nowadays, it is strange to think of Italian cooking without tomatoes, but these, together with bell peppers, potatoes, corn, and chocolate, did not appear on Italian tables until the eighteenth century when they were imported from the New World. American turkey and Yemeni coffee also began to appear in the Italian kitchen. It is curious and interesting that cookbooks at this time began to focus on domestic and regional cooking rather than the extravagant and cosmopolitan dishes prepared by chefs.

To talk about the history of Italian cuisine is somewhat misleading as the country was not unified until 1861. Before that, it consisted of a number of small states and principalities and this, too, has left its mark on Italian cooking. Even in these days of increased mobility, Italians are immensely loyal to their own province, hometown, and even village—in cooking just as much as in every other aspect of life.

Regional traditions

This is hardly surprising as using local produce lies at the very heart of Italian cooking. The south cooks with olive oil, whereas the north is ideal for dairy farming so butter is more traditional. Rice is the north's staple food, whereas the durum wheat grown in the warmer southern climate is used to make pasta. Each region has its own specialties and traditional recipes are passed down through the generations. The Pugliese are called "leaf-eaters" because of the superb dishes made from their magnificent vegetable crops. Piedmont entices gastronomes from across the world with its incomparable white truffles. Lombardy is the home of many of Italy's best-known cheeses from mascarpone to Gorgonzola. Emilia-Romagna is rightly proud of its world-famous *prosciutto di Parma*, Parmesan cheese, and balsamic vinegar. Tuscany, thought by some to produce the best olive oil in the world, is also known for the quality of its meat, poultry, and game, not to mention its vast range of bean dishes that have caused Tuscans to be nicknamed "bean-eaters." Abruzzi is the home of the fiery hot *peperoncino* chile, known locally as the "little devil," while Naples in Campania claims to have invented dried pasta some six centuries ago. Sicily is famous for its sweetmeats and desserts.

SWITZERLAND

AUSTRIA

TRENTINO-ALTO ADIGE

FRIULI-VENEZIA GIULIA

SLOVENIA

VALLE D'AOSTA
Aosta

LOMBARDY

Trento

VENETO

Triest

Milan

Lake Garda

Adige

Venice

Turin

Po

PIEDMONT

EMILIA-ROMAGNA

LIGURIA
Genoa

Bologna

Ligurian Sea

Arno
Florence

Ancona

TUSCANY

THE MARCHE

Perugia

UMBRIA

L'Aquila

Adriatic Sea

Tiber

ABRUZZO

Rome

MOLISE

LAZIO

Campobasso

APULIA

CAMPANIA

Bari

Naples

Potenza

BASILICATA

CALABRIA

Catanzaro

Ionian Sea

Palermo

SICILY

Seasonality and freshness

Italian cooking is undoubtedly shaped by the history of the country and the customs and produce of its regions, but two other, inextricably linked factors play an equally important role—seasonality and simplicity. The quintessential quality of all Italian recipes is the careful combination of a few complementary ingredients at the peak of perfection—fresh mozzarella, superbly ripe tomatoes, and aromatic basil leaves drizzled with virgin olive oil is arguably one of the most delicious salads in the world or perfectly ripe strawberries sprinkled with sugar and aged balsamic vinegar and decorated with mint leaves makes a uniquely mouthwatering dessert.

Seasonality remains a priority—tomatoes, so integral to Italian cooking, must be at the sunshine peak of ripeness, fresh artichoke hearts can be found only in spring, and if you want apricots other than straight off the tree in early summer, then they must be dried when freshly harvested. That is the true taste of Italy.

Italian food today

While regionalism is still acknowledged in Italian gastronomy—everyone knows that ossobucco is a Milanese specialty, saltimbocca comes from Rome, and pizza Margherita was invented in Naples—the cuisine has become more integrated as have the people. The years following World War II saw massive migration from the poor rural communities of the south to the wealthier cities of the north. The migrants brought their culinary traditions with them, enriching those of their new homes, but rural communities were decimated and their culinary traditions began to disappear.

In addition, these years saw an increasing dominance of Anglo-American culture throughout Europe, and Italy was no exception. Fast food, convenience products, and supermarkets all had their effect. However, *campanilismo*—a kind of proud parochialism—runs deep in Italy and the rural communities of the south, where farming rather than industry is the main occupation, held resolutely to their traditions. This, combined with an expanding tourist industry and the phenomenal spread of Italian restaurants in cities throughout the world, meant that the wonderful traditions of authentic traditional country fare were never completely lost.

Antipasti
& First
Courses

Favorite Antipasti

Olive ascolane
Fried Stuffed Olives

30 large, pitted green olives
5–6 oz (150 g) salsiccia
(coarse, spicy sausage)
2 tbsp grated Parmesan
1 tbsp tomato purée
1 egg, beaten
oil for frying
flour for breading
breadcrumbs

Heat the oil in a deep fryer to 350°F (175°C). Rinse the olives with water and dry well. Press the sausage from its skin and combine the meat with the Parmesan and tomato purée. Fill the olives with the mixture and pinch them shut.

Dredge the olives in flour, then dip in the beaten egg and coat with breadcrumbs. Fry in the hot oil until golden brown, then place on paper towels. Serve warm or cold.

Melanzane alla campagnola
Country-Style Marinated
Eggplant Slices

4 eggplants
6 tomatoes
2 garlic cloves
½ bunch parsley
4 tbsp olive oil, plus extra to grease the pan
salt
freshly ground pepper

Wash and trim the eggplants, then cut into slices ⅓ inch (1 cm) thick. Salt them and place in a sieve to drain for 1 hour.

Preheat the oven to 390°F (200°C). Meanwhile, peel and quarter the tomatoes, remove the seeds, and finely dice the flesh. Peel the garlic and mince it along with the parsley. Add this mixture to the tomatoes, then salt and pepper to taste. Stir in 2 tablespoons of the olive oil and let everything marinate briefly.

Pat the eggplant slices dry with paper towels and arrange them next to each other on an oiled baking sheet. Drizzle the remaining olive oil over them, then roast in the oven for 5 minutes on each side.

Brush the eggplant slices with the tomato mixture and stack them up into little towers.

Pomodorini ciliegia ripieni
Stuffed Cherry Tomatoes

generous 1 lb (500 g) cherry tomatoes
7 oz (200 g) feta cheese, diced
2 tbsp olive oil
1 handful basil
salt
freshly ground pepper

Cut the tops off the tomatoes, discard them, then remove the seeds. Cut the feta cheese into small cubes.

Season the inside of the tomatoes with salt and pepper, then stuff them with the cheese cubes. Drizzle the olive oil over them and add more pepper.

Rinse and spin dry the basil. Garnish the tomatoes with individual basil leaves.

Vongole veraci marinate
Marinated Clams

2¼ lb (1 kg) fresh clams
1 onion
2 garlic cloves
7 tbsp (100 ml) olive oil
1 cup (250 ml) dry white wine
1 tbsp finely chopped parsley
juice of ½ lemon
salt
freshly ground pepper
8 scallop shells
(available at fish markets)

Scrub the shells. Soak them in cold water for 1 hour, changing the water several times. Discard any clams that have open shells. Peel the onion and garlic and finely dice them.

Heat 2 tablespoons of the oil in a large pot, and sauté the onions and garlic until translucent. Deglaze with the wine and bring to a boil. Add the clams, cover, and cook on high heat for 3 to 4 minutes, shaking the pot several times.

Remove the clams from the pot with a slotted spoon, discarding any that have not opened. Cut the clam flesh out of the shells and place in a bowl.

Stir together the parsley, lemon juice, and remaining olive oil, and season with salt and pepper. Pour over the clams and let them marinate for 30 minutes. Serve the marinated clams in the scallop shells.

Bruschetta con mozzarella
Bruschetta with
Mozzarella and Tomatoes

4 slices Tuscan country bread
2 garlic cloves
4 tbsp olive oil
5–6 oz (150 g) buffalo mozzarella, sliced
2 tomatoes, sliced
salt
freshly ground pepper
basil leaves to garnish

Toast the bread slices on both sides, either on a grill or under the broiler, until golden brown.

Cut the garlic cloves in half. Rub each slice of bread with the cut side of a halved garlic clove, drizzle with 1 tablespoon of olive oil, then cut in half. Top the bread with sliced mozzarella and tomatoes, salt and pepper, and garnish with basil leaves.

Salvia fritta
Fried Sage Leaves

2 eggs
4 tbsp flour
pinch of salt
⅛ tsp dry yeast
½ cup (125 ml) dry white wine
9 oz (250 g) buffalo mozzarella
32 large sage leaves
olive oil for frying

Separate the eggs. Beat the egg yolks with the flour, salt, yeast, and white wine until smooth. Let the batter rest for 30 minutes. Then beat the egg whites to very stiff peaks and fold into the batter.

Cut the mozzarella into eight slices, then cut each slice in half. Place a piece of mozzarella on sixteen of the sage leaves, top with the remaining sage leaves, and press down.

Heat olive oil in a deep pan or fryer to 350°F (175°C). Dip the sage bundles into the batter one at a time. Fry a few of them at a time in the hot oil until golden brown. Before serving, briefly set on paper towels to remove excess oil.

Funghi sott'olio

Funghi sott'olio
Mushrooms Preserved in Oil

2¼ lb (1 kg) small mushrooms
(champignons, porcini, chanterelles,
honey mushrooms)

1 fresh red chile

1 cup (250 ml) olive oil

7 tbsp (100 ml) white balsamic vinegar

salt

1 small sprig oregano or rosemary

Clean the mushrooms and pat dry with paper towels. Cut the chile in half, remove the core, and cut the flesh into fine strips.

Heat 5 tablespoons of the olive oil in a large pan and brown the mushrooms on all sides until the liquid has evaporated.

Add the chile to the pan and sauté briefly. Deglaze the pan with the vinegar, add salt, then transfer the mushrooms to a bowl. Add the herb and remaining olive oil. Cover and let the mushrooms marinate overnight.

Verdure sottaceto
Vegetables Pickled in Vinegar

For the marinade:

1 cup (250 ml) dry white wine

generous ¾ cup (200 ml) white wine vinegar

7 tbsp (100 ml) olive oil

1 piece lemon peel

5 sprigs parsley

1 celery rib, diced

1 sprig thyme

1 bay leaf

1 garlic clove

10 peppercorns

½ tsp salt

2¼ lb (1 kg) vegetables (carrots, celery,
green beans, asparagus, zucchini,
cauliflower, bell peppers, leeks, onions)

1 tbsp sugar

juice of 1 lemon

salt

In a pan, bring to a boil 2 cups (500 ml) of water and all the ingredients for the marinade. Simmer for 15 minutes.

Cut the vegetables into chunks of equal size. Fill another pot with salted water, add the sugar and lemon juice, and bring to a boil. Cook each vegetable in the water, separately, for 3 to 7 minutes depending on kind and size. Remove the vegetables, drain well, and layer them inside a large canning jar. Pour the boiling hot marinade over them and seal the jar. Marinate the vegetables in the refrigerator for at least two days.

Cipolle all'agrodolce
Pearl Onions in Balsamico

generous 1 lb (500 g) pearl onions
1 garlic clove
2 sprigs thyme
2 bay leaves
2 cloves
5 black peppercorns
1 cup (250 ml) red wine
½ cup (125 ml) balsamic vinegar
1 tsp thyme honey
2 tbsp olive oil

Place the pearl onions and garlic in a saucepan. Add the thyme, bay leaves, cloves, and peppercorns. Pour on the red wine and vinegar and stir in the honey. Bring to a boil and simmer for approximately 25 minutes, or until the pearl onions are soft.

Remove the pan from the stove and let the onions cool in the broth. Discard the thyme, bay leaves, and cloves. Stir in the olive oil.

Fagioli all'agrodolce
Marinated White Beans

1¼ cups (250 g) dried white beans
1 bay leaf
1 garlic clove
4 scallions
1 tbsp lemon juice
3 tbsp white wine vinegar
5 tbsp olive oil
1 tbsp finely chopped parsley
½ cup (50 g) grated Parmesan
salt and pepper

Soak the beans overnight in plenty of water. The next day, cook the beans in the soaking water, adding the bay leaf and garlic to the pot. Bring to a boil, then skim off and cook over low heat until the beans are tender.

Remove the beans from the stove. Discard the garlic and bay leaf, then let the beans cool in the cooking liquid until lukewarm. Trim the scallions and cut into fine strips. Whisk the lemon juice, vinegar, oil, and salt and pepper to make a dressing.

Pour off the liquid from the beans and drain well. Combine the beans with the scallions and dressing and let stand for at least 15 minutes. Sprinkle with the parsley and grated Parmesan before serving.

Bay Leaves

The evergreen bay laurel tree, whose leaves were woven into victory crowns in ancient Roman times, originally came from the Middle East. Bay leaves were equally important for cooking in those days. Fresh or dried bay leaves flavored soups, meat and fish dishes, sauces, and pastas, lending them a tart, slightly bitter taste. But one should refrain from eating the leaves, and not only because of their intense flavor. The leathery leaf is no delicacy, and is therefore most often removed before serving. It is preferable not to use ground bay leaves, because, like most spices, they lose much of their flavor once they are cut, leaving nothing but a bitter taste. For pickling vegetables, fresh bay leaves are far superior to dried ones, because they have a more intense flavor.

Fagioli all'agrodolce

Mozzarella

Nothing represents the colors of the Italian flag so delectably as fresh basil, tender mozzarella, and aromatic tomatoes.

Mozzarella is a fresh, delicate, white cheese with just a hint of sweetness. It is a *pasta filata*, or stretched-curd type of cheese (Italian: *filare*, to pull). As it is being made, the cheese curd is scalded and kneaded or stretched, then shaped into balls, braids, or other regionally typical configurations. It is most often sold fresh, packed in salt water. *Burrielli*, an exceptional delicacy, consists of little mozzarella balls that are stored in milk-filled clay amphoras. Mozzarella has experienced a similar culinary fate to that of Parmesan: both cheeses are famous in nearly every corner of the globe, yet it is mainly only cheap imitations of these Italian specialties that are sold. Authentic *mozzarella di bufala* is produced in the Aversa, Battipaglia, Capua, Eboli, and Sessa Aurunca regions of Campania, and has carried the DOP (Protected Designation of Origin) certification mark since the 1990s. In order to claim DOP status, the cheese must be made from the milk of water buffalo cows that are raised on the open range and nourished with natural feed. Buffalo milk contains significantly more calcium, protein, and fat than the milk of typical dairy cows.

Mozzarella di bufala is a specialty that comes at a price. That is why in many shops you will find the less expensive variety, *mozzarella fior di latte*, which is made from cow's milk and cannot come close to the flavor of the original. The two kinds of mozzarella differ not only in flavor: *mozzarella di bufala* contains over 50 percent more fat, has 45 percent less water than its cow's milk cousin, and, when sliced, reveals a finely layered texture. It is best suited for fillings or for the famous *insalata caprese*, tomato slices with buffalo mozzarella and basil.

Basil

Basil has been cultivated for over 4,000 years. The ancient Greeks called the intensely aromatic plant "the royal herb," and treasured not only its powerful fragrance, but also its healing properties. Basil originally came from Asia. Today there are at least sixty varieties of basil, the most familiar of which are small-leaf Greek basil, and sweet or Italian basil, also called *Basilico genovese*. Both of these have a distinctly different flavor than the Asian and African varieties. When used fresh, delicate green basil leaves from the Mediterranean regions have a slightly peppery, spicy-sweet flavor. These sensitive plants need a lot of sun and plentiful moisture. Liguria has nearly ideal climatic conditions for optimal cultivation, as does Piedmont. When using basil in cooking, it should not be cooked with the rest of the ingredients, but instead should be added at the end of the cooking process. Apropos, basil is a symbol of love in Italy.

Insalata caprese di bufala
Mozzarella with Tomatoes and Basil

generous 1 lb (500 g) vine tomatoes, sliced
1 buffalo mozzarella, ca. 11 oz (300 g), sliced
1 bunch basil
4 tbsp olive oil
salt
freshly ground pepper

Arrange the tomato and mozzarella slices on four plates.

Rinse the basil and shake it dry. Tear off the leaves and sprinkle them over the salad.

Whisk the olive oil with salt and pepper and drizzle over the salad. Traditionally, insalata caprese is made without vinegar, but more and more often, balsamic vinegar is added to the dressing.

Mozzarella in carozza
Breaded Mozzarella Sandwich

1 buffalo mozzarella, ca. 11 oz (300 g)
8 thin slices white bread, with crusts removed
½ cup (125 ml) milk
2 eggs
salt
freshly ground pepper
flour for breading
olive oil for frying

Cut the mozzarella into four slices slightly smaller than the bread. Arrange the cheese on four slices of bread, season with salt and pepper, then cover with the remaining bread and press down lightly. Pour the milk into a flat bowl, briefly turn each sandwich in it, and press the bread firmly against the side of the bowl. Whisk the eggs in a deep dish. Turn the bread in the eggs to coat thoroughly, then coat in flour. Heat an ample amount of olive oil in a deep pan and fry the sandwiches on each side until golden brown. Serve very hot.

Only "happy" water buffalo deliver milk for authentic mozzarella. The largest population of these animals lives in Campania on the Gulf of Naples.

To produce mozzarella, buffalo milk is first combined with rennet. The resulting cheese curd is cut into pieces and placed in a kettle.

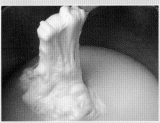

The pieces of curd are then doused with hot water and pulled into strands by hand, using a wooden stick, until they be come a doughy, elastic paste.

The uniform pieces are separated, then pulled into shape, kneaded, and dunked again in hot whey until the desired consistency is achieved.

Stuffed Vegetables

Throughout the Mediterranean region, stuffed vegetables are very popular everyday fare. Fleshy vegetables with firm skins or rinds that can be thoroughly scooped out are best suited for this purpose. They should not be overly ripe, so that they hold their shape when filled and cooked.

The sky is the limit when it comes to the fillings. Raw vegetables such as tomatoes and cucumbers make excellent, flavorful "packaging" for salads with mayonnaise. On the other hand, braised vegetables such as eggplant or zucchini make delicious shells for ground meat or seasoned rice.

Stuffed vegetables are not only suitable as main dishes, but also as antipasti. When served as appetizers, they are often cut into bite-size portions, and can be enjoyed lukewarm or cold.

Pomodori ripieni di tonno
Stuffed Tomatoes

4 large, firm beefsteak tomatoes
5–6 oz (150 g) canned tuna in oil
2 eggs, hard boiled
1 small white onion, finely chopped
4 tbsp mayonnaise
1 tbsp finely chopped parsley
4 lettuce leaves
salt
freshly ground pepper

Wash the tomatoes and cut off the tops, including the stems, for use as lids. Scoop out the core and seeds with a spoon.

Salt the insides of the tomatoes, place upside down in a sieve, and let drain.

Drain the tuna and flake with a fork. Peel and chop the eggs. Combine the onions, tuna, and egg with the mayonnaise and parsley, then add salt and pepper to taste.

Put the filling in the tomatoes, set the tops back on, and arrange the filled tomatoes on the lettuce leaves.

Pomodori ripieni di tonno

First remove the tops from the washed tomatoes and scoop out the core and seeds with a spoon. Only the firm flesh should remain.

Lightly salt the tomatoes to remove some of the liquid. Place them upside down in a sieve and let drain for 10 minutes.

For the stuffing, mix drained canned tuna with mayonnaise, finely chopped hard-boiled eggs, and finely chopped onion and parsley. Season the mixture with salt and pepper.

Finally, stuff the hollow tomatoes with the tuna filling and place the tops over the stuffing to garnish. Arrange the stuffed vegetables on a plate and serve.

Funghi porcini ripieni
Stuffed Porcini Mushrooms

generous 1 lb (500 g) porcini mushrooms
7 tbsp (100 ml) olive oil,
plus extra for greasing
1 small white onion, finely chopped
1 garlic clove, minced
7 tbsp (100 ml) white wine
2 tbsp finely chopped parsley
½ cup (50 g) grated Pecorino Romano
1 tbsp breadcrumbs
salt
freshly ground pepper

Grease a baking dish with olive oil. Clean the porcini. Remove the stems from the caps and finely chop the stems.

Heat half of the olive oil in a large frying pan and sauté the porcini caps over low heat for about 5 minutes. Remove the mushroom caps and place them face down in the baking dish.

Sauté the onion, garlic, and chopped porcini stems in the pan juices for 5 minutes, stirring continuously. Deglaze with the wine, then stir in the parsley. Season with salt and pepper, and simmer for another 5 minutes.

Use the mixture to stuff the porcini caps. Mix the Pecorino Romano and breadcrumbs and sprinkle over the stuffed caps. Drizzle with the remaining olive oil and brown for a few minutes under the broiler.

Cipolle ripiene
Stuffed Onions

4 large onions
1¾ oz (50 g) prosciutto,
cut into fine strips
1 tbsp finely chopped sage
1 tbsp finely chopped oregano
7 oz (200 g) fresh goat cheese
1 egg, beaten
½ cup (125 ml) white wine
generous ½ cup (60 g) grated Parmesan
salt
freshly ground pepper

Preheat the oven to 350°F (175°C). Peel the onions. Bring a pot of salted water to a boil and cook the onions for 10 to 15 minutes. Then refresh them in cold water, let cool a little longer, and cut off the top third for use as a lid. Carefully scoop out the onions with a spoon, leaving a shell about ¹/₃ inch (1 cm) thick. Finely dice the scooped-out flesh.

Combine the diced onion, ham, and herbs with the cheese and egg. Season with salt and pepper. Fill the onion shells with this mixture and top them with the onion lids.

Place the stuffed onions close together in a baking dish and pour the wine over them. Cover the dish with aluminum foil and bake for 30 to 40 minutes. Sprinkle the stuffed onions with the grated Parmesan before serving.

Cipolle ripiene

Fish and Seafood

It should come as no surprise that seafood is a firm fixture of antipasto buffets all along the Italian coastline, even if the crustaceans are no longer coming exclusively from the Mediterranean, but are farmed in Central America and Asia as well. What endures is the Italians' love of Neptune's treasures, accompanied by the ability to conjure up a wealth of delicious dishes with mussels, shrimp, and small fish, ranging from simple to elaborate, with just a few carefully selected ingredients.

A visit to the local fish markets in the small coastal villages of a morning is a must. Not only will you be astonished to discover that there are indeed still fish in Italian waters, you can also enjoy mussels and other seafood in one of the small, local restaurants. Nowhere do they taste as good, for this is where they land in the pot fresh from the sea and are prepared without gimmicks. Add a piece of bread and a glass of wine, and little else is needed for a feeling of all-around well-being.

Bianchetti

Bianchetti, young anchovies and sardines, are a connoisseur's specialty. They are not only tasty, they are healthy, as well, because they are high in omega-3 fatty acids. In Liguria and the Veneto region, the little fish are deep-fried and eaten whole. In the Maremma area, they are cooked with eggs into a frittata or with a thin batter in *frittele* (fritters). In southern Italy, *bianchetti* are thickened into a paste with tomatoes and peperoncini, and spread on toasted slices of bread.

Insalata di mare
Seafood Salad

generous 1 lb (500 g) clams
1 small onion
2 garlic cloves
1 bunch soup vegetables
(mixed root vegetables and herbs)
7 tbsp (100 ml) olive oil
1 cup (250 ml) white wine
14 oz (400 g) small squid, ready to cook
7 oz (200 g) shrimp, shelled
1 celery rib
2 tbsp finely chopped parsley
4 tbsp lemon juice
salt
freshly ground black pepper

Clean the clams under flowing cold water and discard any that are open. Peel and chop the onions and garlic. Finely dice the soup greens (for example, onion, carrot, turnip, and parsley).

Heat 3 tablespoons of the olive oil in a deep pan and lightly sauté the onion, garlic, and soup greens. Pour in the white wine, add the clams, and cook for 10 minutes. Then remove the clams and discard any that have not opened.

Strain the clam broth, bring it to a boil, and cook the squid in it for about 20 minutes. Then add the shrimp and cook for 2 to 3 minutes longer. Strain and drain well.

Chop the celery into thin slices. Scoop out the clam flesh and combine it with the squid, shrimp, celery, and parsley. Season the remaining olive oil with the lemon juice, salt, and pepper, and pour over the salad.

Stir well, cover, and chill in the refrigerator for 2 hours. Remove from the refrigerator 10 minutes before serving.

Wash the fresh sardines, pat dry, and coat with flour. Shake off the extra flour.

Fry the sardines on both sides in olive oil over medium heat until golden brown.

Sarde in saor
Venetian-Style Sardines

2 tbsp currants
4 cups (1 liter) dry white wine
1¾ lb (750 g) fresh small sardines, ready to cook
⅔ cup (150 ml) olive oil
4 onions, cut in thin rings
1 tbsp mixed spice seeds (black pepper, allspice, coriander)
4 bay leaves
1 cup (250 ml) white wine vinegar
2 tbsp sugar
salt and pepper
flour for coating

Soak the currants in 7 tablespoons (100 ml) of the wine for about 10 minutes. Wash the sardines and pat dry. Season inside and out with salt and pepper, coat with flour, and shake off the excess.

Heat 7 tablespoons (100 ml) of the olive oil in a deep pan and fry the fish on both sides, in portions, until golden brown. Remove from the pan and let drain on paper towels.

Gently sauté the onion in the remaining olive oil, pour on the rest of the wine, add the seeds and bay leaves, and bring to a boil. Stir in the vinegar, currants, and sugar, and simmer the broth for 10 minutes on low heat.

Turn half of the sardines into a ceramic bowl and pour on a little of the onion-currant broth. Put in the remaining sardines and spread the rest of the broth over them. Cover the bowl with plastic wrap and let the sardines stand in a cool place for at least 2 days before serving.

Gently simmer the onion rings with bay leaves in olive oil, then cook al dente in white wine.

Season the hot onion broth with vinegar, currants, and sugar, and pour over the fried sardines.

Cozze e vongole passate ai ferri
Broiled Mussels

2¼ lb (1 kg) blue mussels
generous 1 lb (500 g) cockle clams
3 tbsp olive oil
1 bunch soup greens
(mixed root vegetables and herbs),
coarsely chopped
1 onion, chopped
2 garlic cloves, chopped
coarse sea salt
2 tbsp pine nuts
1½ tbsp (25 g) soft butter
2 tbsp grated Parmesan
1 tbsp finely chopped parsley
salt
freshly ground pepper

Clean the mussels and clams thoroughly under cold running water and dispense with any beards. Discard any open clams.

Heat the olive oil in a large pot. Fry the bouquet garni, onion, and garlic in it. Add the clams, cover the pot, and simmer for about 5 minutes, shaking the pot several times during that time. Take the clams out of the pot and let them cool. Discard any clams that are still closed.

Spread a generous amount of sea salt inside a deep baking dish. Break off one half of each blue mussel shell, scoop out the flesh, return it to the shell, and place in the bed of salt. Remove the cockle clam flesh and purée it in a blender with the pine nuts, butter, and Parmesan. Stir in the parsley, then season with salt and pepper.

Cover the mussels with the mixture and broil for approximately 5 minutes.

Carciofi e frutti di mare
Artichokes with Seafood

4–6 small young artichokes
juice of 2 lemons
3 garlic cloves
¼ cup (60 ml) olive oil
½ cup (125 ml) white wine
1 lb (450 g) frozen, pre-cooked
mixed seafood (thawed)
11 oz (300 g) buffalo mozzarella, sliced
salt
freshly ground pepper
butter for greasing

Clean the artichokes, cut the stems to a length of 1½ inches (4 cm), and peel. Remove the tough, outer leaves and slice off the thistles from the inner leaves.

Fill a bowl with 4 cups (1 liter) of water and add the lemon juice. Cut the artichokes lengthwise into thin slices and immediately drop them into the lemon water. Let them soak for 10 minutes, then pour off the water and drain well.

Cut the garlic into slices. Heat the olive oil in a nonstick pan and fry the garlic until golden brown, then remove and discard it.

Sauté the artichoke slices in the olive oil, stirring constantly. Season with salt and pepper, then add the white wine. Cover the pan and gently braise the artichokes on medium heat for about 30 minutes, shaking the pan several times as they cook. During that time, preheat the oven to 440°F (225°C) and butter a baking dish.

Place the artichoke slices in the baking dish and pour on the cooking juices. Add the seafood to the artichokes and top with mozzarella slices. Bake for 20 to 25 minutes, until the mozzarella starts to brown.

Gamberetti olio e limone
Shrimp in Lemon Dressing

generous 1 lb (500 g) cooked shrimp
7 tbsp lemon juice
⅔ cup (150 ml) olive oil
4 lettuce leaves
4 lemon slices
salt
freshly ground white pepper
cayenne pepper

Put the shrimp in a sieve, rinse briefly with running water, and let drain. Whisk salt, white pepper, and a pinch of cayenne into the lemon juice and olive oil. Toss the shrimp in it and marinate briefly. Place the lettuce in four glass bowls and arrange the shrimp on top. Garnish each bowl with one slice of lemon.

Favorite Antipasti with Fish

Acciughe al verde (Piedmont): Pickled anchovies with garlic, parsley, lemon juice, and olive oil.
Baccala mantecato (Veneto): Dried cod with chives, garlic, and oil.
Bottarga (Sardinia): Thin slices of dried, salted tuna roe with olive oil and lemon juice.
Moscardini (Liguria): Tiny squid braised with tomatoes, rosemary, and garlic.
Mussoli in insalata (Friuli-Venezia Giulia): Steamed mussels in lemon juice and olive oil with parsley.
Mustica (Calabria): Salted anchovies in spicy peperoncino marinade.
Pesce scabecciau (Sardinia): Small fish baked in vinegar marinade with garlic, parsley, and tomatoes.
Sfogie in saor (Veneto): Small baked sole, pickled in sweet-sour vinegar with raisins and spices.

Carpaccio

Approximately fifty years ago, the legendary Giuseppe Cipriani created the first carpaccio at Harry's Bar in Venice in honor of the countess Amalia Nani Mocenigo. The noblewoman, a regular guest at his bar, had anemia, and as a result her doctor had recommended that she eat a diet rich in raw meat. Because of the colors that prevail on the plate—red (meat) and white (mayonnaise)—Cipriani named his creation after the renowned Renaissance painter Vittore Carpaccio, who especially prized these colors and used them frequently in his paintings.

These days carpaccio signifies extremely thin slices of raw meat, fish, or vegetables marinated in a little olive oil, lemon, salt, and pepper. Because it is not cooked, it is particularly important that only ingredients of the highest quality be used for carpaccio, ones that have ripened into their own distinctive flavors. If you are not a purist, you can lend additional flavor to carpaccio with arugula, Parmesan, herbs, and garlic.

Carpaccio di finocchi
con finocchiona

Carpaccio di finocchi con finocchiona
Fennel Salami Carpaccio

2 large fennel bulbs
3½ oz (100 g) fennel salami, thinly sliced
juice of 1 lemon and 1 orange
1 tsp flower blossom honey
1 tsp mustard
1 tbsp white wine vinegar
3½ tbsp olive oil
salt and pepper

Trim the fennel and slice it very thin with a mandolin or a food slicer. Decoratively arrange the sliced salami on four plates.

Whisk together the remaining ingredients and pour this dressing over the fennel salami carpaccio. Marinate for 10 minutes or longer before serving.

Carpaccio cipriani
Fillet of Beef Carpaccio

7 oz (200 g) fillet of beef
3 tbsp mayonnaise
1 tbsp milk
1–2 tsp lemon juice
Worcestershire sauce
salt
freshly ground pepper

Wrap the beef fillet in plastic wrap, place in the freezer, and let it harden.

Stir the mayonnaise, milk, and lemon juice into a thick cream and season with the Worcestershire sauce, salt, and pepper. Cut the frozen fillet into wafer-thin slices and lay them on a chilled serving platter. Use a spoon to drizzle the mayonnaise sauce over the meat in a gridlike pattern.

Carpaccio di porcini

Carpaccio di porcini
Porcini Mushroom Carpaccio

2 bunches arugula
14 oz (400 g) small porcini mushrooms
juice of 2 lemons
5 tbsp olive oil
2 tbsp balsamic vinegar
2 oz (50 g) piece of Parmesan
salt
freshly ground pepper

Wash the arugula, removing any wilted leaves and thick stems, then shake dry. Place it on four plates.

Clean the porcini, slice them thinly lengthwise, and immediately place in the lemon juice, turning to coat both sides. Arrange the sliced mushrooms on the arugula. Whisk the olive oil with the vinegar, add salt and pepper, and drizzle over the porcini. Top with thinly shaved Parmesan.

Carpaccio cipriani

Carpaccio di pesce spada
Swordfish Carpaccio

3½ oz (100 g) seaweed
1 avocado
juice of 3 lemons
1 tsp red peppercorns
generous 1 lb (500 g) swordfish fillet, frozen
4 tbsp olive oil
salt
freshly ground white pepper

Wash the seaweed, discarding any hard stems, then break it into bite-size pieces and set on paper towels to dry. Cut the avocado in half lengthwise. Twist the halves in opposite directions to separate the flesh from the pit. With a spoon, scoop the flesh from the skin in one piece, cut it into thin slices, and immediately sprinkle with some of the lemon juice. Crush the peppercorns in a mortar.

With a food slicer, cut the frozen swordfish into wafer-thin slices and place them on four plates. Season with the remaining lemon juice, crushed peppercorns, salt, and white pepper. Arrange the seaweed and avocado slices decoratively on the fish, drizzle with the olive oil, and serve immediately.

Bresaola

Bresaola is a special kind of air-dried beef made from certain meaty, high-quality cuts of beef in Valtellina, a valley in the northern Italian Alps. The meat is cured with a little salt and spices such as pepper, cinnamon, nutmeg, garlic, bay leaf, and juniper berries, and then left to age in the cool air. Thanks to favorable climatic conditions, the meat remains tender and moist even after the drying process is completed. It has a distinctive dark red color, and is exceptionally soft and mild. In 1998, a consortium was founded to safeguard the name *Bresaola della Valtellina*, to protect its traditional production, and to support marketing and distribution efforts.

Bresaola is cut into gossamer-thin slices and usually served as an appetizer, either on its own or with olive oil and pepper in the style of carpaccio.

Bresaola con rucola
Bresaola with Arugula

1 handful arugula
11 oz (300 g) bresaola, thinly sliced
⅓ cup (80 ml) olive oil
coarsely ground pepper
1 lemon, cut into wedges

Wash the arugula, spin it dry, and remove any coarse stems. Cut the leaves into fine strips.

Lay out the bresaola slices on four plates. Drizzle the olive oil over them, turning the plates as you do so, to distribute the oil evenly.

Grind pepper over the bresaola and sprinkle with the arugula strips. Garnish with lemon wedges.

Selected pieces of beef are cut and then rubbed with seasonings and salt.

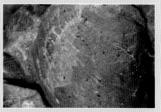

The meat is air cured for an entire month, during which it is turned in the seasonings every two days.

The meat is then tied up like a rolled roast and left to air dry for a few months.

During the aging process, a natural, protective layer of white mold develops on the bresaola.

Ham

Ham is the best part of the pig, and it is not only Italian producers and consumers who are of that opinion. The flavorful, air-dried hindquarters of the pig have been treasured since ancient times. The Italian word *prosciutto* comes from the Latin *perexsutum*, which means "dried." The Romans were intimately familiar with the secrets of producing fine ham. They also knew that the low humidity, wind, and climate at the outskirts of the northern Italian Alps were ideal for preservation of meats, and even improved the quality of the meat itself.

To this very day, the time-tested method of preparing cured ham has not changed very much in Italy. The back leg or haunch (with or without the bone) is first cured in salt and herbs for a period of time, and then air dried (not smoked). The tangy air circulates throughout the drying rooms and lends the ham its unique flavor, which, like the climate, differs slightly from region to region.

The most famous Italian cured raw hams are undoubtedly *prosciutto di Parma* and *prosciutto di San Daniele*. As DOP hams (*Denominazione d'Origine Protetta*, or Protected Designation of Origin), both have enjoyed protected status within the European Union for years, and a consortium oversees them to maintain the high quality standards of these specialties.

Prosciutto con melone e fichi
Prosciutto with Melon and Figs

½ *honeydew melon*
8 *fresh figs*
7 oz (200 g) *prosciutto*

Quarter the melon, remove the seeds and peel, and cut into slices. Wash the figs, pat them dry, and cut crosswise, so that they open like flowers.

Place the figs in the middle of a plate and add the melon slices. Arrange the prosciutto decoratively around the fruit.

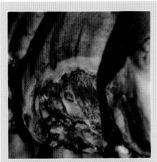

Prosciutto di San Daniele

San Daniele ham can look back on a long and illustrious history. It was the Celts who laid the foundations for fruitful agriculture at this location in the region of Friuli. And the ancient gravestone of a butcher, found in Portogruaro near Venice, bears a perfectly depicted San Daniele ham, including the hoof. To this day, this very special prosciutto is made from pork legs with the entire leg bone intact. In order to bear the designation *prosciutto di San Daniele*, the pigs must be born in specific regions of Italy, and they must be raised, fed, and slaughtered according to regulations. Only sea salt is rubbed on the fresh pork legs, which are then air dried. The aging process takes at least twelve months. Finished hams have an intense flavor and distinct aftertaste. Wrapped around grissini breadsticks, the very thinly sliced ham is shown to best advantage.

Focaccia alla salvia

Focaccia

Focaccia is a very popular flatbread in Liguria. When baked to perfection, it is soft inside and crispy outside. In earlier times, it used to be eaten as a meal in itself with fresh figs. Today it is available around the clock, an indispensable part of breakfast, snack time, or a savory bite to eat with aperitifs. In Genoa and the surrounding area, numerous *panetterie* and *focaccerie* offer this delicious flatbread from the early hours of the morning onward. And many locals eat the bread directly from the bag while walking down the street.

The medieval town of Recco in Liguria is considered the birthplace of cheese focaccia. A long time ago, a certain Mr. Manuelina Maggio is supposed to have baked this special flatbread for the first time. His recipe: a simple yeast dough with oil produced in the Ligurian Riviera, filled with *stracchino*, the rich soft cheese native to this region.

Since 1976, the gastronomic consortium of Recco has organized events featuring *focaccia col formaggio*, which has been a protected trademark since 1995. Each year on the fourth Sunday in May, Recco celebrates the Focaccia Festival, called the *Sagra della focaccia*. Throughout the day, bakers hand out their delicious flatbread free of charge.

Focaccia alla salvia
Focaccia with Sage

1½ oz (40 g) compressed fresh yeast or
2 envelopes active dry yeast
1 pinch sugar
3 cups (400 g) flour, plus extra for dusting
1 tsp salt
½ cup (125 ml) olive oil,
plus extra for greasing
12 fresh sage leaves, finely chopped
2 tbsp coarse sea salt

Crumble the yeast into 1 cup (250 ml) of luke-warm water and dissolve, along with the sugar. Stir in 4 tablespoons of the flour, cover, and let the resulting sponge proof in a warm place for 15 minutes.

Sift the remaining flour into a bowl, make a hollow in the center, and pour the sponge into it. Add the salt and 3–4 tablespoons of the olive oil and knead into a silky dough. Shape it into a ball, cover, and let rise in a warm spot for 1 hour, or until doubled in volume.

Grease a baking sheet with olive oil and preheat the oven to 480°F (250°C). Vigorously knead the dough again, working in the sage leaves. On a floured surface, roll out the dough to a thickness of about ¼ inch (2 cm), then place it on the baking sheet. Gently press down on the dough with your fingers to form many little indentations. Brush it with the remaining olive oil, scatter sea salt over the top, and bake for 20 to 25 minutes. Cut into squares to serve.

Focaccia con cipolle
Focaccia with Onions

1½ oz (40 g) compressed fresh yeast or
2 envelopes active dry yeast
1 pinch sugar
3 cups (400 g) flour, plus extra for dusting
1 tsp salt
½ cup (125 ml) olive oil,
plus extra for greasing
2 onions, cut into thin rings
¾ cup (100 g) black olives, pitted
2–3 garlic cloves, finely chopped
1 tbsp coarse sea salt
2 tsp crushed peppercorns

Crumble the yeast into 1 cup (250 ml) of luke-warm water and dissolve, along with the sugar. Stir in 4 tablespoons of the flour, cover, and let the resulting sponge proof in a warm place for 15 minutes.

Sift the remaining flour into a bowl, make a hollow in the center, and pour the sponge into it. Add the salt and 3–4 tablespoons of olive oil and knead into a silky dough. Shape it into a ball, cover, and set in a warm spot to rise for 1 hour, or until doubled in volume.

Grease a baking sheet with olive oil and preheat the oven to 480°F (250°C). Vigorously knead the dough again. On a floured surface, roll out the dough to a thickness of about ¼ inch (2 cm), then place on the baking sheet and prick with a fork. Cover with the onions and olives and sprinkle with garlic. Drizzle on the remaining olive oil, season with sea salt and pepper, and bake for about 20 minutes.

To make focaccia dough, first dissolve the yeast in lukewarm water along with a little sugar.

Stir in a small amount of flour, cover and leave the sponge to rise in a warm, draught-free spot.

Then knead the sponge with the other ingredients by hand or in a food processor.

Put the dough in a bowl, cover it and leave it to rise until it has doubled in volume.

On a floured surface, roll out the dough into an oval about ¼ inch (2 cm) thick.

Place it on a greased baking tray and cover with onion rings and olives.

Pizza

When asked why their pizzas taste so much better than pizzas anywhere else, Italians do not have to think for long. It is still the wood-fired ovens that lend the dough its very special flavor. A genuine pizza oven is dome shaped, and its interior walls are lined with ovenproof (heat-resistant) tiles. In the small village of Maiano near Naples, these ovens have been handmade out of clay from the Sorrento Peninsula since the fifteenth century, using a special technique.

On the stone floor of the pizza oven, a wood fire burns directly on the baking surface. But the fire hardly produces any smoke, because cherry or olive wood are burned. The flames heat up the tile walls, while the distinctive shape of the oven provides for even distribution of the heat. When fully heated, the burning wood is pushed to the rear of the oven to make room for the pizzas. The glowing embers keep the temperature of the oven at a minimum of 750°F (400°C). At this incredible temperature, the pizza bakes very quickly. In less than a minute, the bottom of the dough is crisp, the tomatoes are not yet dry, the mozzarella is perfectly melted, and the healthy fatty acids in the olive oil have not yet been destroyed.

Pizzette

Basic Pizza Dough

1½ oz (40 g) compressed fresh yeast or 2 envelopes active dry yeast
½ tsp sugar
3 cups (400 g) flour, plus extra for dusting
1 tsp salt
3 tbsp olive oil

Crumble the yeast into a small bowl and sprinkle with the sugar. Add ½ cup (125 ml) of lukewarm water, then stir to dissolve the yeast and sugar. Cover with a clean kitchen towel and proof in a warm spot for 30 minutes. Sift the flour into a large bowl. Make a hollow in the center and pour the yeast mixture, salt, olive oil, and 5–7 tablespoons of water into it. Knead everything into a smooth, silky dough, then shape it into a ball. Dust the ball with a little flour, cover, and set aside in a warm place to rise for an additional hour, or until doubled in volume.

Pizzette
Small Pizzas

1½ oz (40 g) compressed fresh yeast or 2 envelopes active dry yeast
½ tsp sugar
3 cups (400 g) flour, plus extra for dusting
1 tsp salt
¼ cup (60 ml) olive oil, plus extra for greasing
generous 1 lb (500 g) tomatoes
1 radicchio
3½ oz (100 g) bacon, cut into strips
6 tbsp (50 g) pine nuts

Crumble the yeast into a small bowl and sprinkle with the sugar. Add ½ cup (125 ml) of lukewarm water, then stir to dissolve the yeast and sugar. Cover with a clean kitchen towel and proof in a warm spot for 30 minutes. Sift the flour into a large bowl. Make a hollow in the center and pour the yeast mixture, salt, 3 tablespoons of olive oil, and 5–7 tablespoons of water into it. Knead everything into a smooth, silky dough, then shape it into a ball. Dust the ball with a little flour, cover, and set aside in a warm place to rise for about 1 hour, or until doubled in volume.

Preheat the oven to 390°F (200°C) and grease two baking sheets with olive oil. Peel and quarter the tomatoes, remove the seeds, and cut into small dice. Trim the radicchio and break it into bite-size pieces.

Divide the dough into 12 equal pieces. Form each one into a ball, flatten, and place the rounds on the baking sheets. Top with the diced tomato and bacon and drizzle on the remaining oil. Bake for 15 minutes, then sprinkle the radicchio and pine nuts over the *pizzette* and bake for another 5 minutes.

Pizza di patate
Apulian Potato Pizza

1¾ lb (750 g) potatoes
1 tsp salt
3 tbsp flour
5 tbsp (70 ml) olive oil, plus extra for greasing
14 oz (400 g) canned peeled tomatoes
¾ cup (100 g) black olives
12 anchovies in oil
5–6 oz (150 g) feta cheese, diced
1 onion, cut into rings
2 garlic cloves, finely chopped
½ tsp rosemary
½ tsp dried oregano
freshly ground pepper

Bring a pot of salted water to a boil and cook the potatoes. Drain, rinse them in cold water, peel, and put through a potato press while still warm. Stir in the salt, flour, and 2 tablespoons of the olive oil, and let the mixture cool.

Preheat the oven to 430°F (220°C). Grease a springform pan (11 inches/28 cm in diameter) with olive oil. Drain the tomatoes and cut them into small pieces. Press the potato dough into the pan, creating a rim. Spread the tomatoes, olives, anchovies, feta cheese, onion, and garlic on the dough. Sprinkle with rosemary, oregano, and pepper, then bake for approximately 30 minutes.

Pizza Margherita

1 pizza dough
(see recipe on page 28)
⅓ cup (75 ml) olive oil,
plus extra for greasing
2 small onions, diced
14 oz (400 g) canned diced tomatoes
18 oz (50 g) canned tomato sauce
1 tsp oregano
14 oz (400 g) mozzarella
salt and pepper
flour for dusting
basil leaves to garnish

Heat 4 tablespoons of the olive oil and sauté the onions until translucent. Add both kinds of tomatoes and the oregano, and season with salt and pepper. Cook the sauce for about 30 minutes on medium heat.

Preheat the oven to 435°F (225°C) and grease four round pizza pans with olive oil.

Divide the dough into four equal portions and roll them into circles on a floured surface. Place the circles of dough on the pizza pans.

Thinly slice the mozzarella. Brush the dough with the tomato sauce, cover with mozzarella slices, and drizzle on the remaining olive oil. Bake for about 20 minutes, then garnish with basil leaves and serve immediately.

Pizza alla marinara
Mariner's Pizza

1 pizza dough
(see recipe on page 28)
24 oz (800 g) canned diced tomatoes
3–4 garlic cloves, finely chopped
1 tbsp oregano
⅓ cup (50 g) capers
¼ cup (100 g) black olives
7 oz (200 g) Bel Paese cheese, grated
3 tbsp olive oil, plus extra for greasing
flour for dusting
salt
freshly ground pepper

Preheat the oven to 435°F (225°C) and grease four round pizza pans with olive oil. Divide the dough into four equal portions and roll them into circles on a floured surface. Place the circles of dough on the pizza pans.

Distribute the tomatoes on the dough. Season with the garlic, oregano, salt, and pepper. Scatter on the capers and olives and sprinkle with the grated cheese. Drizzle on the olive oil, then bake the pizzas for about 20 minutes.

Pizza quattro stagioni
Four Seasons Pizza

1 pizza dough
(see recipe on page 28)
1 tbsp butter
7 oz (200 g) mushrooms, sliced
4 tomatoes
7 oz (200 g) cooked ham
7 oz (200 g) mozzarella
4 artichoke hearts in oil
16 black olives
1 tsp oregano
4 tbsp olive oil, plus extra for greasing
flour for dusting
salt and pepper

Preheat the oven to 435°F (225°C) and grease four round pizza pans with olive oil. Heat the butter and sauté the mushrooms for 10 minutes. Peel and quarter the tomatoes, remove the seeds, and cut into small dice. Cut the ham into small pieces. Thinly slice the mozzarella. Quarter the artichoke hearts.

Divide the dough into four equal portions and roll them into circles on a floured surface. Place the circles of dough on the pizza pans.

Distribute the tomatoes and mozzarella evenly on the pizzas. Cover one quarter of each of the pizzas with one of the following toppings: mushrooms, ham, artichokes, and olives. Season with the oregano, salt, pepper, and drizzle with the olive oil. Bake for about 20 minutes.

Favorite Salads

Insalata di arance
Orange Salad

4 oranges
1 red onion
2 tbsp finely chopped parsley
4 tbsp olive oil
salt
freshly ground pepper

Peel the oranges and remove the pith, then slice in rounds. Lay them out in a fan pattern on a plate. Peel and halve the onion, and thinly slice one half. Finely chop the other and combine with the parsley.

Sprinkle the sliced and chopped onions over the orange slices, season with a little salt and pepper, and drizzle olive oil over the salad. Cover with plastic wrap and marinate for 1 hour in the refrigerator. Remove from the refrigerator 5 minutes before serving.

Insalata di tonno e fagioli
Bean Salad with Tuna

2 cups (400 g) white beans, cooked
4 scallions, finely chopped
1 fresh red chile, finely chopped
2 celery ribs, finely diced
2 tbsp lemon juice
6 tbsp olive oil
6 oz (170 g) canned tuna in oil
1 tbsp finely chopped parsley
salt
freshly ground pepper

Mix together the cooked beans, scallions, chile, and celery. Whisk together the lemon juice and olive oil to make a dressing, season with salt and pepper, and pour it over the salad. Set aside to marinate for 15 minutes.

Drain the tuna fish and break into bite-size chunks. Stir the tuna and parsley into the bean salad.

Olio e sale alla barese
Tomato Salad with Cucumber, Onion, and Bread

1 small cucumber, peeled
2 beefsteak tomatoes
1 white onion
4 tbsp olive oil
2 tbsp white wine vinegar
2 slices of white country bread
salt
freshly ground pepper

Thinly slice the cucumber and tomatoes and place them in a salad bowl. Slice the onion into fine rings, then toss them with the cucumber and tomatoes.

Whisk together the olive oil and vinegar, season with salt and pepper, and pour over the salad. Marinate for 20 minutes.

Toast the bread slices on both sides under a broiler or in the oven until golden brown, then cut into bite-size pieces. Toss them into the salad and serve immediately.

Insalata di carciofi
Artichoke Salad

8 small purple artichokes
3 tbsp lemon juice
1 cup (250 ml) white wine
½ tsp salt, plus extra to season
7 tbsp (100 ml) olive oil
2 garlic cloves, finely chopped
1 small red onion, finely chopped
2 tbsp tarragon vinegar
6 basil leaves
freshly ground pepper

Remove the hard outer leaves from the artichokes and cut away the upper half of the tender inner leaves. Shorten the stems to 2 inches (5 cm) and peel them. Immediately place the artichokes in a saucepan with water and the lemon juice.

Add the white wine, salt and 2 tablespoons of the olive oil to the pan and bring to a boil. Cover and cook on medium heat for 20 to 25 minutes. Then take the artichokes out of the water, let cool slightly, and cut them in half lengthwise.

Stir the garlic and onion with 2 tablespoons of the artichoke cooking water, the tarragon vinegar, and salt and pepper to taste. Mix in the remaining olive oil. Cut the basil leaves into fine strips. Lay the artichoke halves face up in a bowl, pour the dressing over them, and sprinkle the basil on top. Serve while moderately warm.

Radicchio alla vicentina
Radicchio Salad

14 oz (400 g) radicchio di Chioggia
3½ oz (100 g) pancetta
1 tbsp olive oil
2 tbsp balsamic vinegar
salt
freshly ground pepper

Trim and wash the radicchio, then spin it dry. Tear the leaves into bite-size pieces and arrange on four plates. Finely dice the pancetta.

Heat the olive oil in a pan and fry the pancetta until crispy. Deglaze with the vinegar and season with salt and pepper. Pour the pancetta and pan juices over the radicchio and serve immediately.

Panzanella
Bread Salad

| 14 oz (400 g) day-old |
| Tuscan country bread |
| 1 small cucumber |
| 2 small white onions |
| 7 tbsp (100 ml) olive oil |
| 2–3 tbsp red wine vinegar |
| generous 1 lb (500 g) tomatoes, sliced |
| 1 handful arugula |
| salt |
| freshly ground pepper |

Cut the bread into slices about ¾ inch (2 cm) thick and soak them in a bowl of cold water for no more than 10 minutes.

Peel the cucumber, cut it in half lengthwise, and remove the seeds. Thinly slice the cucumber halves. Slice the onions into fine rings. Thoroughly squeeze the water out of the bread slices and tear into bite-size pieces.

Heat half of the olive oil in a nonstick pan and sauté the bread, turning it constantly. Remove from the heat and let cool slightly.

Whisk together the remaining olive oil, the vinegar, salt, and pepper. In a larger bowl, combine the cucumbers, tomatoes, onions, toasted bread, and dressing.

Rinse the arugula, pat it dry, and remove any wilted leaves and coarse stems. Line four bowls with the arugula and arrange the bread salad on it. In the original version, bread salad was covered and left to marinate in a cool place for several hours. Nowadays, it is usually served immediately so that the toasted bread remains crispy.

Asparagi all'olio e aceto balsamico
Asparagus Salad
with Balsamic Vinegar

| 14 oz (400 g) each: green asparagus, |
| white asparagus |
| ⅓ cup (75 ml) olive oil |
| 2 tbsp balsamic vinegar |
| salt |
| freshly ground pepper |
| parsley leaves to garnish |

Wash and trim the asparagus. Lightly peel the white asparagus and remove the woody ends from both kinds. Cut all the asparagus stems to the same length, bundle them in portions, and place in a deep, narrow pot. Fill the pot two-thirds full with cold water, salt lightly, cover, and bring to a boil. Cook until the asparagus is tender yet still crisp.

Remove the asparagus from the water and drain well. Whisk together the olive oil, vinegar, salt, and pepper to make a dressing. Lay the asparagus on a serving plate, pour the dressing over it, and garnish with parsley. Serve while moderately warm.

Rucola

Rucola is an annual wild herb with long, dark green leaves that is known by many names in English: arugula, Italian cress, rocket, or rucola. The variety with delicate leaves is a familiar salad ingredient, whereas the broad-leaved version is mainly used to produce oil. The more mature types of arugula taste slightly sour and a little peppery. Most cultivated types of arugula that are available today have a predominantly nutty, mild flavor. Although it looks robust at first glance, arugula is very delicate and wilts easily. It is most often used in combination with other salad greens, often with fruit. Arugula with bresaola or prosciutto and Parmesan is a very popular appetizer, but arugula is being used more and more on pizzas or finely cut and mixed into pasta dishes.

Insalata con rucola e parmigiano
Arugula and Parmesan Salad

| 2 handfuls arugula |
| 1 small fennel bulb |
| ⅓ cup (75 ml) olive oil |
| 2 tbsp balsamic vinegar |
| 3½ oz (100 g) Parmesan |
| 6 tbsp (50 g) pine nuts |
| salt |
| freshly ground pepper |

Rinse the arugula, pat it dry, and remove any wilted leaves or coarse stems. Divide the leaves among four plates. Halve the fennel bulb, slice it thinly, and spread some over the arugula on each plate.

Whisk together the olive oil, balsamic vinegar, salt, and pepper and drizzle over the salad. Top the salad with shaved Parmesan. Dry-roast the pine nuts in an ungreased pan until golden brown, then sprinkle over each serving of salad.

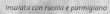
Insalata con rucola e parmigiano

Soups

The Italians often say that soups are the true test for aficionados of great food. To prepare a good soup requires time, care, and attention, beginning with shopping for just the right ingredients. The ingredients that go into the soup pot vary from region to region, but one thing is the same throughout Italy: the broth is made from a piece of meat and never from a bouillon cube. Every homemaker and every butcher knows the best cuts of meat for a hearty stock: breast, back, stomach, shoulder, and tongue. Poultry broth is made not only from soup chickens, but also from duck, goose, and capon meat.

All soups are based on two basic recipes: *minestra in brodo*, which is a broth with vegetables, noodles, or rice; and *zuppa*, a thick soup that is frequently poured over a slice of bread. *Minestrone* is the most famous Italian soup, and it can be found in countless variations. In the northern regions of Italy it is prepared with rice and Parmesan, in Tuscany with beans and fresh olive oil, and in the south with tomatoes and garlic.

Zuppa has peasant roots. It was made from whatever was in season, as well as leftovers from slaughtering or fishing. Some delicious, filling examples are spelt soup, Tuscan cabbage soup, hearty tripe stew, and fish soup, which is often served as a main course.

Minestrone

1 cup (200 g) dried white beans
2 potatoes
2 carrots
1 celery rib
1 onion, finely chopped
1 garlic clove, finely chopped
4 tbsp olive oil
2 small zucchinis
2 small tomatoes
1 cup (150 g) peas
scant ⅔ cup (125 g) pearl barley
4–5 oz (125 g) smoked bacon,
cut in fine strips (optional)
½ cup (50 g) grated Parmesan
1 tbsp finely chopped basil
salt
freshly ground pepper

Soak the beans overnight. Wash, trim, and peel the potatoes, carrots, and celery, then cut into small dice. Heat the olive oil in a large pot and fry the onion and garlic until translucent. Add the diced vegetables to the pot and brown briefly.

Pour the soaking water off the beans. Add the beans and 8 cups (2 liters) of water to the pot, cover, and simmer on low heat for 1 hour.

Thinly slice the zucchini. Peel and quarter the tomatoes, remove the seeds, and dice. Add the zucchini, tomatoes, peas, pearl barley, and the bacon (if using) to the soup. Season with salt and pepper and cook for an additional 20 to 25 minutes, stirring occasionally. Prior to serving, sprinkle on the Parmesan and basil. Older recipes called for minestrone to be simmered for up to 4 hours, but today many people prefer their vegetables a bit crisper.

Panata
Bread Soup

7 oz (200 g) plum tomatoes
1 celery rib
7 tbsp (100 ml) olive oil
1 garlic clove, finely chopped
2 bay leaves
4 slices day-old Tuscan country bread
4 eggs
½ cup (50 g) grated Parmesan
1 tbsp finely chopped parsley
salt
freshly ground pepper

Peel and quarter the tomatoes, remove the seeds, and dice. Finely dice the celery. Heat 4 tablespoons of the olive oil and sauté the vegetables and garlic. Add 4 cups (1 liter) of water and the bay leaves and season with salt and pepper. Let the broth simmer for about 30 minutes, then pour it through a sieve into a larger pot.

Remove the crusts from the bread. Cut the bread into bite-size pieces and sauté in the remaining olive oil. Divide the cubes among four soup bowls. Bring the vegetable broth to a boil once more, crack the eggs into it one at a time, and cook them in the hot broth. Place 1 poached egg in each bowl and pour hot broth over it. Sprinkle with Parmesan and parsley and serve immediately.

Pappa al pomodoro
Tomato Soup

2¼ lb (1 kg) tomatoes
4 tbsp olive oil
4 garlic cloves, finely chopped
3¼ cups (750 ml) meat stock
4 slices Tuscan country bread
a few basil leaves to garnish
salt
freshly ground pepper

Peel and quarter the tomatoes, remove the seeds, and cut into cubes. Heat the olive oil and fry the garlic. Add the diced tomatoes and cook for 5 minutes. Pour in the meat stock and let the mixture thicken on medium heat until the desired consistency is reached. Season with salt and pepper.

Toast the bread slices on both sides under a hot broiler or in the oven until golden brown, then cut them into cubes. Add the bread cubes to the soup just before serving and garnish with basil leaves.

Ribollita
Tuscan Bean Soup

¾ cup (150 g) dried white beans
3½ oz (100 g) pancetta
½ savoy cabbage, cut into strips
2 carrots, sliced
14 oz (400 g) canned peeled tomatoes
4 cups (1 liter) meat stock
1 tbsp chopped oregano
1 onion
4 slices day-old Tuscan country bread
½ cup (50 g) grated Parmesan
2 tbsp olive oil
salt
freshly ground pepper

Soak the beans overnight in 4 cups (1 liter) of water. The next day, bring to a boil in the soaking water and cook for 1 hour.

Finely dice the pancetta and render it in a pot, then sauté the cabbage and carrots in the fat. Mash the tomatoes with a fork and add them to the pot. Pour in the stock and season with the oregano and salt and pepper.

When the beans have cooked, pour off the cooking water, add the beans to the soup, and cook for another 15 minutes. Slice the onion into very thin rings. Preheat the oven to 480°F (250°C).

Toast the bread, cut it in half, and place in four ovenproof soup bowls. Pour the soup over the bread and top with onion rings. Sprinkle with Parmesan and drizzle with the olive oil. Bake until the onion rings are brown.

Favorite Soups

Canederli allo speck in brodo
Bacon Dumpling Soup

5 day-old rolls
½ cup (125 ml) lukewarm milk
3½ oz (100 g) smoked bacon, diced
1 small onion, diced
2 tbsp finely chopped parsley
2 eggs
4 cups (1 liter) hearty meat stock
salt
freshly ground pepper
freshly grated nutmeg

Cut the rolls into fine slices, pour the warm milk over them, and soak for 10 minutes.

Render the bacon in an ungreased pan, then add the onions and sauté. Stir in half of the parsley. Remove from the heat and let it cool. Then add the mixture to the bread, add the eggs, and knead well. Season the dumpling mixture to taste with salt, pepper, and nutmeg. Set it aside for 30 minutes.

With wet hands, form small dumplings from the dough. Bring a large pot of salted water to a boil. Add the dumplings and simmer for 10 minutes on low heat until done. Bring the meat stock to a boil. Transfer the dumplings to the stock and steep them in the broth briefly, but do not cook further. Sprinkle with the remaining chopped parsley before serving.

Zuppa di pesce
Fish Soup

1¾ lb (750 g) mixed fresh fish, ready to cook
2 tbsp olive oil
1 Bermuda onion, finely chopped
2 garlic cloves, finely chopped
1 leek, cut into thin rings
1 tbsp tomato paste
4 tomatoes
1 tsp fennel seeds
1 tbsp finely chopped parsley
salt
freshly ground pepper

Wash the fish thoroughly. Bring 4 cups (1 liter) of water with 1 teaspoon salt to a boil, add the fish, and simmer on low heat for 10 minutes, but do not cook any longer than that. Remove the fish from the broth, pat it dry, and set aside to cool.

Heat the olive oil in a pot and sauté the onion, garlic, and leek until the onions are translucent. Stir in the tomato paste, then add the fish broth and bring to a boil.

Peel and quarter the tomatoes, remove the seeds, and dice. Grind the fennel seeds with a mortar and pestle. Add the tomatoes and ground fennel seeds to the soup and cook for 10 minutes. Skin the fish, fillet it, and cut into bite-size pieces. Warm the fish in the soup. Season with salt and pepper to taste. Serve the soup sprinkled with parsley.

Cipollata
Onion Soup

5 tbsp olive oil
2 oz (50 g) smoked bacon, diced
1¾ lb (750 g) white onions, cut into thin rings
18 oz (500 g) canned tomato purée
2 eggs
6 tbsp (40 g) grated Parmesan
8 basil leaves, cut into strips
salt
freshly ground pepper

Heat the olive oil in a pot and render the bacon in it. Add the onions and sauté on low heat, stirring continuously, until they are translucent. Do not let them brown. Stir in the tomato purée and add 2 cups (500 ml) of water. Season with salt and pepper, cover, and simmer for about 1 hour. Stir frequently and add water as needed, but be careful that the soup does not become too thin.

Whisk the eggs with the Parmesan. Remove the onion soup from the stove and stir in the egg-and-cheese mixture. Serve sprinkled with the basil.

Minestra di farro
Spelt Soup

2 tbsp olive oil
1 small onion, finely chopped
1 carrot, diced
1 celery rib, diced
3 tomatoes, peeled and diced
6 cups (1.5 liters) meat stock
generous 1⅓ cups (200 g) spelt flour
3½ oz (100 g) cooked ham
1 tbsp each: grated Parmesan, pecorino
salt
freshly ground pepper

Heat the olive oil in a soup pot and sauté the onion and vegetables in it, then pour in the meat stock. Bring to a boil and cook for about 1 hour.

Pass the soup through a sieve and bring to a boil once more. Season with salt and stir in the spelt flour. Cook for another 25 minutes on low heat, stirring frequently.

Cut the ham into narrow strips, then stir the ham and cheeses into the soup. Add salt and pepper to taste and serve immediately.

Favorite Pasta Dishes

Tagliolini al tartufo
Tagliolini with White Truffle

14 oz (400 g) tagliolini
7 tbsp (100 g) butter
1 small white truffle
salt

Bring a large pot of lightly salted water to a boil. Add the pasta and cook according to package instructions until al dente.

Meanwhile, melt the butter, but be careful not to let it brown.

Clean the truffle with a dry, soft brush. Drain the pasta thoroughly, then distribute it on four plates. Pour the melted butter over each serving. With a truffle grater, finely shave the truffle over the pasta.

Linguine con salsa di pesce
Linguine with Fish Sauce

14 oz (400 g) fish fillets, such as perch or cod
1¼ lb (600 g) tomatoes
1 onion
4 tbsp olive oil
12 oz (350 g) linguine
1 tbsp finely chopped parsley
flour for coating
salt
freshly ground pepper
basil leaves to garnish

Wash the fish fillets, pat them dry, and coat in flour. Peel and quarter the tomatoes, remove the seeds, and dice. Peel the onion, then cut it in half and slice thinly.

Heat the olive oil in a pan and fry the fish on both sides until golden brown, then remove from the pan and keep warm. Sauté the onions in the oil until translucent, then add the tomatoes. Season with salt and pepper, cover the pan, and simmer on low heat for about 10 minutes.

In the meantime, bring a large pot of lightly salted water to a boil. Add the pasta and cook according to package instructions until al dente. Drain the pasta and toss it with the tomato sauce and parsley while the pasta is still dripping wet. Cut the fish into bite-size pieces and blend into the pasta. Cover and briefly let the flavors mingle. Serve on warmed plates garnished with basil leaves.

Tagliatelle

As if the numerous types of pasta were not confusing enough, the exact same pasta can also have up to ten different names, depending on the region and manufacturer! Luckily, classic tagliatelle have the same name throughout Italy. Oftentimes they are available as both dry and fresh egg noodle products.

Tuscan *pappardelle* are the widest tagliatelle. The linguistic origin of these delicious noodles is anything but genteel. This Tuscan word originally meant "to fill one's gullet," and it is also used in this sense in Boccaccio's *Decameron*.

One of the most popular kinds of egg noodles, tagliatelle are a good ⅓ inch (8 mm) wide. Their name comes from the Italian verb *tagliare*, "to cut." They are usually available rolled into small nests or spirals. They initially came from Bologna, and go perfectly with meat sauces.

In the vicinity of Rome, the somewhat more slender, thicker tagliatelle are called *fettuccine*, and in Liguria, *trenette*. They are just as delightful with a flavorful pesto as with cream or butter sauces containing vegetables, fish, or seafood.

Tagliarellini are slightly more than ⅛ of an inch wide, about 4 mm. Green and white *tagliarellini* are the basis for the classic pasta dish *paglia e fieno* ("straw and hay").

Tagliolini, the most delicate of egg noodles, are just 1 mm wide and taste best with just a little bit of butter and white truffles.

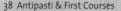

Penne all'arrabbiata
Spicy Penne

generous 1 lb (500 g) tomatoes
2 tbsp olive oil
3½ oz (100 g) pancetta, diced
1 onion, finely chopped
2 garlic cloves, finely chopped
2–3 dried red chiles
14 oz (400 g) penne rigate
⅔ cup (75 g) grated Pecorino Romano
salt

Peel and quarter the tomatoes, remove the seeds, and cut into small dice. Heat the olive oil in a deep pan and fry the pancetta in it. Add the onion and garlic and fry until the onions are translucent. Then add the diced tomatoes and whole chiles and let the sauce simmer on low heat for a while. As soon as it reaches the desired level of spiciness, remove the chiles from the pan.

Bring a large pot of lightly salted water to a boil. Add the pasta and cook for half the time stated in the package instructions, then drain, reserving some of the pasta cooking water.

Mix the penne, 2 tablespoons of the Pecorino Romano, and 3–4 tablespoons of pasta water into the tomato sauce and finish cooking the pasta in the sauce, stirring frequently. Serve on warmed plates sprinkled with the remaining Pecorino Romano.

Rigatoni all'amatriciana
Rigatoni with Bacon and Onions

3 tomatoes
2 tbsp olive oil
3½ oz (100 g) pancetta, diced
2 small white onions, finely chopped
1 small, dried red chile, finely chopped
salt
12 oz (350 g) rigatoni
½ cup (60 g) grated Pecorino Romano

Peel and quarter the tomatoes, remove the seeds, and dice. Heat the olive oil in a pan and fry the diced pancetta until crisp, then remove from the pan and keep warm. Sauté the onion and chile in the bacon fat. Add the tomatoes, salt lightly, and simmer for 10 minutes.

In the meantime, bring a large pot of lightly salted water to a boil. Add the pasta and cook according to package instructions until al dente. Drain the water and tip the pasta into a preheated bowl. Combine it thoroughly with the pancetta, tomato sauce, and Pecorino Romano. Serve immediately.

Ziti con salsiccia
Ziti with Sausage

9 oz (250 g) salsiccia (Italian sausage)
2 yellow bell peppers
2 tomatoes
2 tbsp olive oil
1 white onion, finely chopped
2 garlic cloves, finely chopped
1 cup (250 ml) white wine
1 tbsp oregano, finely chopped
12 oz (350 g) ziti
salt
freshly ground pepper

Skin and slice the sausage. Cut the bell peppers in half, remove the cores, and cut into strips. Peel and quarter the tomatoes, remove the seeds, and cut into small dice.

Heat the olive oil in a deep pan and sauté the onions and garlic until the onions are translucent. Add the sliced sausage and peppers and continue to cook, stirring. Add the diced tomatoes, pour in the wine, then season with the oregano and pepper to taste. Simmer for 15 to 20 minutes on low heat.

In the meantime, break the pasta into bite-size pieces. Bring a large pot of lightly salted water to a boil. Add the pasta and cook according to package instructions until al dente. Drain the pasta and combine with the sauce. Cover and let it stand for 1 or 2 minutes. Serve on warmed plates.

Spaghetti alla Carbonara

14 oz (400 g) spaghetti
4 eggs
4 tbsp heavy cream
½ cup (50 g) grated Parmesan
½ cup (50 g) grated Pecorino Romano
1 tbsp butter
5–6 oz (150 g) pancetta, finely diced
salt
freshly ground pepper

Bring a large pot of lightly salted water to a boil. Add the pasta and cook according to package instructions until al dente.

Meanwhile, stir together the eggs, cream, and cheeses in a bowl. Add salt and pepper.

Melt the butter in a large pan and fry the pancetta until crispy. Drain the spaghetti and add it to the pan while still dripping wet. Pour the cheese sauce over it. Remove the pan from the stove. Toss the pasta in the sauce until the eggs begin to thicken but are still creamy. Serve on warmed plates, sprinkled with freshly ground pepper.

Spaghetti aglio, olio e peperoncino
Spaghetti with Garlic, Oil, and Peperoncino

14 oz (400 g) spaghetti
7 tbsp (100 ml) olive oil
4–6 garlic cloves, finely chopped
2–3 dried chile peppers
2 tbsp finely chopped parsley
salt
freshly ground pepper
⅔ cup (75 g) grated Parmesan

Bring a large pot of lightly salted water to a boil. Add the pasta and cook according to package instructions until al dente.

In a deep pan, heat the olive oil and sauté the garlic and whole chiles in it. As soon as the desired spiciness is reached, remove the chiles from the pan. For a very spicy dish, you can leave the chiles in the garlic oil.

Drain the spaghetti, add it to the deep pot while still dripping wet, and mix with the hot garlic oil and parsley. Season with pepper and serve on warmed plates with the Parmesan on the side.

Spaghetti al pomodoro
Spaghetti with Tomato Sauce

1¼ lb (600 g) tomatoes
4 tbsp olive oil
1 pinch sugar
14 oz (400 g) spaghetti
1 tbsp finely chopped basil leaves
salt
freshly ground pepper
⅔ cup (75 g) grated Parmesan or pecorino cheese

Peel and quarter the tomatoes, remove the seeds, and dice. Then heat the olive oil in a large pan and cook the tomatoes. Season with the sugar, salt, and pepper, and simmer on low heat for about 20 minutes.

Bring a large pot of lightly salted water to a boil. Add the pasta and cook according to package instructions until al dente. Drain the spaghetti and combine it with the tomato sauce while still dripping wet. Serve on warmed plates sprinkled with basil, with the cheese on the side.

Bucatini alla puttanesca
Bucatini with Tomatoes, Capers, and Olives

¾ cup (100 g) black olives, pitted
5 anchovies in oil
4 tbsp olive oil
2 tbsp tomato paste
28 oz (800 g) canned peeled tomatoes
7 tbsp (60 g) small capers
salt
freshly ground pepper
14 oz (400 g) bucatini pasta

Cut the olives into quarters. Finely chop the anchovies. Heat the olive oil in a pot, stir in the tomato paste, and cook it briefly. Crush the tomatoes with a fork, then add to the pot. Stir in the olives, anchovies, and capers, and let the sauce simmer for 20 minutes on low heat. Season to taste with salt and pepper.

Bring a large pot of lightly salted water to a boil. Add the pasta and cook according to package instructions until al dente. Drain the bucatini and mix it into the sauce while still dripping wet. Serve immediately on warmed plates.

Fish, Meat & Vegetables

Favorite
Fish Dishes

Trotelle ai funghi porcini
Trout Fillets
with Porcini Mushrooms

8 trout fillets
1 tbsp chopped tarragon
2 cups (500 ml) white wine
generous 1 lb (500 g) porcini mushrooms
7 tbsp (100 g) butter
1 small onion, finely chopped
1 tbsp chopped thyme
salt
freshly ground pepper

Wash the trout fillets, pat them dry, and rub with salt and pepper. Place the fish in a bowl, sprinkle with the tarragon, and pour ½ cup (125 ml) of wine over them. Cover the bowl and marinate for 30 minutes.

Meanwhile, wipe the porcini mushrooms with a damp cloth, trim the stems, and cut into ½-inch (1-cm) thick slices. Heat half of the butter and sauté the onion until translucent. Add the mushrooms and sauté, stirring, until all the liquid has evaporated. Pour in the rest of the wine and season with salt, pepper, and the thyme. Simmer on low heat for 10 minutes.

Melt the rest of the butter in a large, nonstick pan. Remove the trout fillets from the marinade, pat them dry, and sauté in hot butter for 3 minutes on each side. Then pour in the marinade and bring it to a boil. Serve the mushrooms with the fish.

Trote affogate
Trout in White Wine

4 fresh brook trout, ready to cook
⅓ cup (75 ml) olive oil
1 white onion, finely chopped
2 garlic cloves, finely chopped
1 tbsp finely chopped parsley
1 cup (125 ml) white wine
salt
freshly ground pepper
flour

Wash the trout, pat them dry, and season with salt and pepper. Coat in flour and tap off the excess.

Heat the oil in a large pan and place the trout in the pan. Add the onion, garlic, and parsley. Fry the trout for 4 minutes on each side on medium heat.

Pour in the wine and cook the trout on low heat for an additional 10 minutes. Pour the cooking juices over the fish before serving.

Brodetto friulano
Friulian Fish Stew

2¼ lb (1 kg) mixed freshwater fish
(for example, eel, tench, or perch),
ready to cook

1 white onion
2 garlic cloves
2 carrots
2 celery ribs
9 oz (250 g) tomatoes
2 tbsp olive oil
2 cups (500 ml) fish stock
2 bay leaves
1 tbsp balsamic vinegar
4 slices white bread
salt
freshly ground pepper

Wash the fish, pat it dry, and cut into bite-size pieces. Season with salt and pepper. Finely dice the onion and garlic. Cut the carrots and celery into fine dice. Peel and quarter the tomatoes, remove the core, and cut into fine dice.

Heat the olive oil in a deep pan and sauté the onions and garlic. Add the carrots and celery, browning lightly. Mix in the tomatoes, pour in the fish stock, and add the bay leaves. Simmer together for 10 minutes.

Add the fish to the stew and cook on low heat for about 10 minutes. Remove the bay leaves and season the stew with salt, pepper, and the balsamic vinegar. Toast the white bread and place each slice in a deep bowl. Ladle the fish stew over the toast and serve immediately.

Triglie di fango al pesto
Red Mullet with Parsley Pesto

| 4 red mullet or red snapper, |
| 11 oz (300 g) each, ready to cook |
| juice of 1 lemon |
| 7 tbsp (60 g) pine nuts |
| 2 garlic cloves, chopped |
| 1 tsp salt, plus extra to season |
| 2 bunches parsley, finely chopped |
| ⅔ cup (150 ml) olive oil |
| 2 tbsp grated Parmesan |
| freshly ground pepper |
| flour for coating |
| lemon wedges to garnish |

Wash the fish, pat it dry, and sprinkle with the lemon juice. Season the fish inside and out with salt and pepper.

Dry-roast the pine nuts in an ungreased pan until golden brown. Remove from the stove and let cool.

Grind the garlic and salt with a large mortar and pestle. Add the pine nuts and parsley, and grind into a paste. Gradually work in 7 tablespoons of the olive oil. Mix in the Parmesan last, adding a little water if necessary.

Heat the remaining oil in a large pan. Coat the fish in flour and shake off the excess, then fry the fish in the hot oil for 4 to 5 minutes per side. Remove from the pan and place on four warmed plates. Serve topped with the parsley pesto and garnished with lemon wedges.

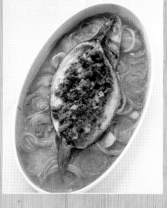

Sogliola ai carciofi
Sole with Artichokes

8 small purple artichokes
juice of 1 lemon
½ cup (125 ml) olive oil
4 garlic cloves, thinly sliced
1 cup (250 ml) dry white wine
1⅔ cups (400 ml) bouillon
1¾ lb (800 g) fillet of sole
salt
freshly ground pepper
flour for coating
1 tbsp finely chopped parsley

Clean the artichokes, shorten the stems to about 1½ inches (4 cm), and peel them. Remove the tough outer leaves and trim the hard thorns from the remaining leaves. Mix the lemon juice and some water in a bowl. Slice the artichokes lengthwise and immediately put them in the lemon water. Marinate for a short time, then pour off the liquid and dab the artichokes dry.

Heat 6 tablespoons of the olive oil in a large pan and sauté the artichokes. Add the garlic and sauté until golden brown. Deglaze with the wine, pour in the bouillon, and add salt and pepper. Simmer for 20 to 25 minutes, then remove from the stovetop.

Season the fish fillets with salt and pepper, coat in flour, and shake off the excess. Heat the remaining oil and fry the fish on both sides. Serve the fish over the artichokes, sprinkled with the chopped parsley.

Branzino ripieno
Stuffed Sea Bass

⅓ oz (10 g) dried porcini mushrooms
3½ oz (100 g) cooked shrimp, shelled
1 tbsp chopped thyme
1 egg
1–2 tbsp breadcrumbs
1 sea bass, ca. 3 lb (1.4 kg), ready to cook
1 Bermuda onion, cut into thin rings
2 tbsp butter
1 cup (250 ml) white wine
oil for greasing
freshly grated nutmeg
salt
freshly ground pepper

Soak the porcini in ⅔ cup (150 ml) of hot water for 15 minutes, then pour the liquid through a fine sieve and reserve it for later. Drain and finely chop the porcini.

Preheat the oven to 350°F (175°C) and grease a baking dish with oil. Finely chop the shrimp and mix with the mushrooms, thyme, egg, and breadcrumbs. Season with nutmeg. Wash the fish, pat it dry, and rub inside and out with salt.

Stuff the fish with the mushroom-shrimp mixture. Close the opening with wooden skewers. Place the onion rings in the bottom of the baking dish, then lay the fish on them. Put little pats of butter on top of the fish. Pour in the reserved soaking water and half the wine. Bake the fish for about 45 minutes, gradually adding the rest of the wine during that time.

Transfer the fish to a warmed platter. Pour off the cooking juices, season with salt and pepper, and serve with the fish.

Branzino alla pugliese
Braised Sea Bass with Zucchini

1 sea bass, ca. 2¼ lb (1 kg), ready to cook
2 firm potatoes
2 large zucchini
2 garlic cloves, finely chopped
½ tsp salt, plus extra to season
⅔ cup (150 ml) olive oil
2 tbsp finely chopped parsley
1 cup (250 ml) white wine
freshly ground pepper

Preheat the oven to 355°F (180°C). Wash the fish, pat it dry, and season inside and out with salt and pepper. Peel and thinly slice the potatoes. Wash the zucchini and thinly slice them lengthwise.

Grind the garlic and salt with a mortar and pestle, then stir them into the oil and mix with the parsley. Pour half of the oil mixture into a baking dish and place the zucchini slices in it. Season with pepper. Lay the fish on the zucchini. Arrange the potato slices so they fan out over the fish and drizzle the rest of the oil mixture over them.

Bake the fish for 15 minutes. Then pour in the white wine and braise for an additional 30 minutes. Serve in the baking dish.

Coda di rospo al rosmarino
Monkfish with Rosemary

1¾ lb (800 g) monkfish (without the head)
⅔ cup (150 ml) olive oil
3 sprigs rosemary
3 garlic cloves, peeled
salt
freshly ground pepper

Detach the monkfish fillets from the backbone, wash them, pat dry, and season with salt and pepper.

Heat the olive oil slightly in a deep pan. Add the rosemary and garlic and sauté for several minutes. Then remove the garlic and put the fish in the pan. Fry on medium heat for 3 minutes on each side. Serve the monkfish over a vegetable risotto.

Involtini di pesce spada
Swordfish Roulades

4 long, thin swordfish slices,
ca. 7 oz (200 g) each
lemon juice for sprinkling
5 tbsp olive oil
1 small onion, finely chopped
1 garlic clove, finely chopped
2 tbsp finely chopped parsley
2 tbsp grated Pecorino Romano
2 tbsp breadcrumbs
½ cup (125 ml) white wine
1 tbsp chopped thyme
salt
freshly ground pepper
cayenne pepper
flour for coating

Wash the fish, pat it dry, and sprinkle with lemon juice. Heat 2 tablespoons of olive oil in a pan and sauté the onion and garlic. Mix in the parsley, then remove from the stove and let cool.

Stir the Pecorino Romano and breadcrumbs into the onion mixture. Season with salt and cayenne pepper. Spread the mixture on the fish slices, roll them up, and secure with wooden skewers.

Heat the remaining olive oil in a separate pan. Coat the fish roulades in flour and fry on all sides for 10 to 12 minutes on low heat. Then remove from the pan and keep warm. Deglaze the pan drippings with wine and season the sauce with thyme, salt, and pepper. Serve the roulades with the sauce.

Involtini di mullo alle erbe
Red Mullet with Herb Stuffing

20 red mullet or
red snapper fillets (with skin)
juice of 1 lemon
2 garlic cloves
1 small onion
3 tbsp olive oil, plus extra for greasing
2 tbsp finely chopped parsley
8 sage leaves, finely chopped
10 thin slices uncooked ham, halved
½ cup (125 ml) white wine
4 tbsp breadcrumbs
salt
freshly ground pepper

Preheat the oven to 390°F (200°C) and grease a baking dish with olive oil. Wash the fish fillets, pat them dry, and season with salt and pepper. Lay them on a platter and sprinkle with the lemon juice.

Mince the garlic and onion. Heat 1 tablespoon of the olive oil in a pan and sauté the garlic, onion, and herbs. Remove from the stove and let cool slightly.

Place the fillets skin side down on a work surface. Spread some of the herb and onion mixture over each one, then lay a half slice of ham on top. Roll up the fillets and secure with wooden skewers.

Place the roulades in the baking dish side by side. Bring the wine to a boil, then pour it over the fish. Sprinkle breadcrumbs over the top and drizzle on the remaining oil. Bake for 15 minutes.

Coda di rospo al rosmarino

Involtini di mullo alle erbe

Tonno fresco al forno
Baked Tuna

1½ lb (700 g) tuna steak
2 tbsp lemon juice
2 bay leaves
several sprigs fennel greens
4 shallots, diced
7 tbsp (100 ml) olive oil
1 cup (250 ml) dry white wine
salt
freshly ground pepper
flour for coating

Preheat the oven to 350°F (175°C). Wash the tuna, pat it dry, and season with salt and pepper. Sprinkle it with the lemon juice, then coat in flour and tap off the excess.

Place the fish in a baking dish and lay the bay leaves and fennel greens on top of it. Scatter the diced shallots around the fish. Drizzle with the olive oil and pour in the white wine.

Cover the dish with aluminum foil. Bake the tuna for 40 minutes, removing the aluminum foil for the last 10 minutes. Cut the fish into four pieces of equal size and serve with the shallots.

Tonno all'alloro
Tuna with Bay Leaves

4 fresh tuna steaks, 9 oz (250 g) each
8 tbsp (120 ml) olive oil
juice of 1 lemon
12 bay leaves
salt
freshly ground pepper

Wash the tuna and pat it dry with paper towels. Whisk together 5 tablespoons of the olive oil, the lemon juice, and salt and pepper. Brush the tuna steaks with the dressing.

Crush the bay leaves several times to release their essential oils. Stack the tuna steaks on top of one another with the bay leaves in between them. Wrap the fish in plastic wrap and chill in the refrigerator for about 3 hours.

Heat the remaining olive oil in a large pan. Remove the plastic wrap and bay leaves from the fish, then fry the fish steaks in oil for about 5 minutes per side.

Coda di rospo al vino bianco
Monkfish in White Wine Sauce

8 small monkfish fillets
5 tbsp olive oil
1 onion, finely chopped
2 garlic cloves, finely chopped
2 celery ribs, diced
2 tbsp finely chopped parsley
1 cup (250 ml) white wine
salt
freshly ground pepper
flour for dusting

Wash the fish fillets and pat dry. Preheat the oven to 390°F (200°C).

Heat 2 tablespoons of the olive oil in a pan and sauté the onions, garlic, and celery. Stir in the parsley and then transfer the vegetables to a baking dish.

Season the fish fillets with salt and pepper, then dust lightly with flour. Heat the remaining oil in a pan and fry the fish briefly on both sides. Then remove the fish from pan and place it on the vegetables. Pour the pan juices over it and add the wine. Bake for 10 to 15 minutes, until done.

Tonno fresco al forno

Filetti di sogliola al cartoccio
Fillet of Sole in Parchment

4 large sole fillets
⅓ cup (50 g) pitted black olives
1 tbsp finely chopped oregano
2 tbsp finely chopped parsley
3 tbsp olive oil, plus extra for greasing
2 tbsp lemon juice
salt
freshly ground pepper

Preheat the oven to 355 °F (180°C). Wash the fish fillets and pat them dry. Finely chop the olives and combine them with the oregano, parsley, and olive oil.

Grease four sheets of parchment paper with olive oil and lay one sole fillet on each. Season with salt, pepper, and lemon juice, then spread the olive-herb mixture over the fish. Enclose the fish fillets in parchment paper, being sure to seal the packets tightly. Bake the fish for 6 to 7 minutes. Serve in parchment paper.

Cooking in Parchment

From very early in history, our ancestors began to wrap vegetables, meat, fish, and poultry in a protective covering of leaves or clay and then cook them gently and slowly.

Wrapping food in something serves two functions. First, it protects the flavoring on the inside and prevents the food from drying out. The meal stews in its own juices and retains valuable nutrients, its unique flavor, and original shape. Also, unhealthy by-products of roasting are prevented from developing by this method. This gentle means of cooking is especially well suited to fish.

Parchment paper has two qualities that are ideal for cooking: it does not get too hot, and it "breathes," which supports the unfolding of flavors during the cooking process. Parchment paper was developed specially for this gentle cooking method, but simple waxed paper can also be used, in layers of three sheets and well oiled, because it must not become saturated. Caution is advised: the oven temperature must not exceed 375°F (190°C) or the paper can catch fire.

Shrimp

Whether it is tiny Bay shrimp, prawns, or jumbo shrimp, these delicious creatures taste best when they are freshly caught and boiled, grilled, or baked right in their shells. Diners encountering shrimp for the first time may wonder how best to maneuver these armored delicacies. The easiest way is to use one's fingers. Even in the best restaurants, this method is entirely customary.

Since the head is simply unpalatable, start by removing it and setting it aside. Then bend the armored shell outward along the stomach and detach the meat from the shell. If the dark vein along the back of the shrimp is still visible, it can be removed with the point of a knife. If no extra plates have been provided, just slide the discarded parts to the edge of the plate.

Now nothing stands in the way of delicious eating. The shelled shrimp are taken in the hand, dipped into a sauce or dip, and eaten. The little bowl of lemon water that is served with them in many Italian restaurants is intended for washing your hands after the meal.

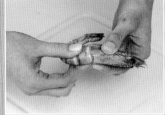

Pick up the shrimp with your hand, remove the head, and set it aside. It is not edible.

With your fingers, remove the shell from the stomach outward.

Cut along the back of the shrimp with a sharp knife to devein.

Dip the shelled shrimp in the sauce with your fingers. Enjoy!

Gamberoni arrabbiati
Shrimp Arrabbiata

generous 1 lb raw shrimp
10 tbsp (145 ml) olive oil
1 fresh red chile, finely chopped
2 tbsp lemon juice
2½ tbsp Italian brandy
2 garlic cloves
generous 1 lb (500 g) tomatoes, diced
½ cup (125 ml) white wine
salt
freshly ground pepper
several small basil leaves

Prepare the shrimp as described above. Stir 6 tablespoons of the olive oil together with the chile, lemon juice, and brandy. Peel the garlic and press it into the seasoned oil. Marinate the shrimp in it for 1 hour.

Heat the remaining olive oil in a pan and sauté the shrimp for about 3 minutes per side. Remove them from the pan and keep warm. Cook the tomatoes in the pan oil and deglaze with the wine. Put the shrimp back in the pan, then season the sauce with salt and pepper. Serve garnished with basil leaves.

Gamberoni alla griglia
Grilled Shrimp

20 raw jumbo shrimp
3 large garlic cloves
7 tbsp (100 ml) olive oil
⅛ teaspoon cayenne pepper
1 tsp dried oregano
1 lemon

Soak four wooden skewers in water. Wash the shrimp and pat them dry. Peel the garlic and press it into the olive oil. Stir in the cayenne pepper and oregano. Place the shrimp in a bowl and pour the garlic oil over them. Cover the bowl and marinate the shrimp in the refrigerator for 4 hours, turning once. Place five shrimps on each of the wooden skewers, and grill on a charcoal grill or broil in the oven for 5 minutes per side. Cut the lemon into wedges and serve with the shrimp.

Crayfish

Italian rivers and brooks were once filled with crayfish, which were popular, everyday fare. However, their populations decreased drastically as water pollution became increasingly prevalent. Today these freshwater relatives of lobster are mainly imported from China, Scandinavia, Poland, and Turkey. They taste best from May through August, and may be sold only live or canned. In the case of cooked crayfish, if the tail is rolled inward, that signals that the crayfish was fresh when cooked. The edible portions are the meat from the tail and claw.

Fritto misto
Fried Seafood

11 oz (300 g) fresh anchovies
14 oz (400 g) seppioline (small squid),
ready to cook
11 oz (300 g) small raw shrimp
scant 1¼ cups (150 g) flour
½ tsp salt
2 tbsp olive oil
2 egg whites
freshly ground white pepper
oil for frying
lemon wedges to garnish

Wash the anchovies, squid, and shrimp and drain well. Cut the squid in half. Mix the flour, salt, olive oil, generous ¾ cup (200 ml) of luke-warm water, and some pepper into a smooth dough. Beat the egg whites until semi-firm and fold them into the dough. Let it rest for 10 minutes.

Heat frying oil to 355°F (180°C). Dip the anchovies, squid, and shrimp into the batter, one at a time, and fry in portions until golden brown. Drain briefly on paper towels and serve with lemon wedges!

Sorrento Lemons

In the seventeenth century, Jesuits on the Sorrento Peninsula and in the Massa Lubrense municipality on the Amalfi Coast began to cultivate a lemon with especially superb qualities, the *limone di massa* or Sorrento lemon, which differs from other lemons in both shape and flavor.

These shiny, bright yellow, oval lemons are characterized by very juicy fruit that has both considerable acidity and a touch of sweetness.

Sorrento lemons now carry the IGP stamp of quality (Protected Geographical Indication). Their pleasant tartness harmoniously rounds out the flavor of fish and seafood.

Veal

Lean, juicy veal is easy to digest and especially rich in high-quality protein. Veal is finely marbled, free of tendons, and delicately textured. It has a certain firmness to the touch. Due to its higher price, veal was once prepared mainly on feast days.

Both male and female calves are butchered, most often between the ages of five and six months. The animal's age and the type of feed it ate determine the color of the meat. Calves that were raised organically and were already let out to pasture have light to dark red meat. Milk-fed calves that were nourished only with milk or milk substitutes have whitish pink meat.

Many Italian veal recipes typically involve wrapping or layering the meat with ham, pancetta, or strips of bacon so that the veal does not become too dry during cooking. Among the most famous dishes are *vitello tonnato*, cooked veal served cold with tuna mayonnaise; *ossobuco*, veal shank that is sliced and braised with bones and marrow; delicious *involtini*, delicate, gently braised roulades; and many different kinds of cutlets.

Scaloppine al limone
Lemon Cutlets

4 thin veal cutlets, 5–6 oz (150 g) each
2 tbsp olive oil
4 tbsp lemon juice
2 tbsp butter
2½ tbsp dry white vermouth
salt
freshly ground pepper
sugar

Wash the cutlets, pat them dry, then press them as flat as possible with the ball of your hand. Lay the cutlets in a shallow bowl. Whisk together the oil and lemon juice and drizzle it over the veal. Cover the bowl and marinate for 30 minutes.

Remove the meat from the marinade, drain, and pat dry with paper towels. Melt the butter in a deep pan and brown the cutlets on both sides. Remove from the pan, season with salt and pepper, and keep them warm. Deglaze the pan with the marinade, stirring to loosen the pan drippings, and add the vermouth. Let the sauce reduce slightly, then season it to taste with salt, pepper, and sugar. Serve the cutlets in the sauce.

Saltimbocca alla romana
Roman Sage Cutlets

8 small, thin veal cutlets,
2–3 oz (75 g) each
8 slices coppa di Parma,
or substitute prosciutto di Parma
16 sage leaves
generous ¾ cup (200 ml) dry white wine
flour for coating
butter for frying
salt
freshly ground pepper

Pound the veal cutlets flat. Place a slice of ham and 2 sage leaves on each cutlet, fold them over, and secure with toothpicks. Then coat with a little flour and shake off any excess.

Melt butter in a large skillet and fry the cutlets on high heat for about 2 minutes per side. Season with salt and pepper, and drizzle with a little of the wine. As soon as the wine reduces, transfer the cutlets from the pan to a warmed platter.

Deglaze with the rest of the wine and stir to loosen the pan drippings. Pour through a sieve and pour over the cutlets.

Scaloppine al limone

Lay the veal cutlets between two layers of plastic wrap and gently pound them flat.

Top each cutlet with 2 sage leaves and a slice of ham.

Fold the veal cutlets together and fasten them with toothpicks.

Saltimbocca alla romana

Involtini in umido

Involtini in umido
Veal Roulettes with Ham

8 thin veal cutlets, 3½ oz (100 g) each
½ cup (50 g) grated pecorino cheese
8 thin slices prosciutto di San Daniele
2 tbsp butter
2 tbsp olive oil
1 onion, finely chopped
1 garlic clove, finely chopped
1 tbsp tomato paste
½ cup (125 ml) Marsala
½ cup (125 ml) veal stock
2 tomatoes, diced
1 small sprig sage
flour for coating
salt and pepper

Pound the cutlets thin between two layers of plastic wrap and place them side by side on a work surface. Season with salt and pepper. Sprinkle the pecorino over them and top each one with a slice of prosciutto. Roll up the cutlets and secure with toothpicks, then salt and pepper the roulettes and coat with flour.

Heat the butter and oil in a pan and brown the roulettes on all sides. Remove from the pan and set aside. Sauté the onion, garlic, and tomato paste in the same pan. Deglaze with the wine, stirring to loosen the pan drippings, and pour in the stock. Add the veal roulettes, tomatoes, and sage to the pan and bring to a boil. Cover and cook on low heat for 20 minutes. Then remove the veal from the pan and keep warm on a serving platter. Remove the sage from the sauce, bring it to a boil, and season with salt and pepper. Pour the sauce over the veal roulettes.

Costolette alla milanese
Milanese Veal Chops

4 veal chops, 7 oz (200 g) each
2 eggs
1 cup (100 g) breadcrumbs
¼ cup (60 g) clarified butter
1 lemon
flour for coating
salt and pepper

Wash the chops, dab them dry, and rub with salt and pepper. Whisk the eggs. Coat the chops first in flour, then in whisked egg, and finally in breadcrumbs. Press the breading firmly in place.

Heat the clarified butter in a large pan, add the chops, and fry on medium heat for 5 to 6 minutes per side, until golden brown. Cut the lemon into wedges and serve with the veal chops.

Ossobuco alla milanese
Milanese-Style Ossobuco

4 slices veal shank, each ca. 1½ inches (4 cm) thick
3½ tbsp (50 g) butter
½ cup (125 ml) white wine
14 oz (400 g) canned tomato purée
1 garlic clove
1 tbsp grated lemon peel
2 tbsp finely chopped parsley
flour for coating
salt
freshly ground pepper

Wash the meat slices and pat dry with paper towels. Then rub with salt and pepper, coat with flour, shaking off any excess.

Melt the butter in a deep pan and brown the veal slices on both sides. Deglaze the pan with the wine, then reduce some. Stir in the tomato purée and season with salt and pepper. Cover the pan and stew the meat on low heat for at least 1½ hours, turning the slices over several times in the tomato sauce as they cook. When the meat begins to separate from the bone, it is done. Finely chop the garlic and combine it with the lemon peel and parsley. Sprinkle over the sliced meat just before serving.

Beef

Tournedos alla Rossini are still famous today and unite three extravagant products on a single plate: fillet of beef, foie gras, and truffles. There are two versions of the story explaining the genesis of the recipe. According to the first, the chef at La Maison Doree Restaurant invented the dish and dedicated it to Rossini. The second version goes like this: when Rossini's chef wanted to try out the new recipe, the maestro required him to prepare it in the dining room so that he and his guests could watch. But the chef explained that it would embarrass him to cook in front of all those people, to which Rossini responded, "Very well then—just turn your back to me."

Tournedos alla Rossini
Tournedos à la Rossini

4 thick beef tenderloin fillets
2 tbsp olive oil
2 tbsp butter
4 slices white bread, toasted
4 slices pâté de foie gras
4 tbsp. Madeira
1 small truffle
salt
freshly ground pepper

Tie the fillets into rounds with kitchen twine. Heat the oil and butter and brown the meat on medium heat for about 3 minutes per side. Season with salt and pepper. Cut each slice of toast into the shape of a tournedo, place the meat on it, and set on a warmed platter. Top with pâté de foie gras. Deglaze the pan with the Madeira and pour over the meat. Thinly grate the truffle over the tournedos.

Brasato alla milanese
Milanese-Style Roast Beef

Serves six

2¼ lb (1 kg) beef roast
2 garlic cloves
1 carrot
2 celery ribs
1 kohlrabi
2 onions
2 tbsp olive oil
2 tbsp butter
1 bay leaf
1 small sprig thyme
1 clove
1¼ cups (300 ml) Barolo or other strong red wine
generous 1 lb (500 g) tomatoes
1¼ cups (300 ml) meat stock
3 tbsp finely chopped parsley
salt
freshly ground pepper

Wash the meat and pat it dry. Peel and slice the garlic. Cut into the meat with a sharp knife and insert the garlic slices into the openings. Season the meat with salt and pepper. Wash or peel and finely dice the carrot, celery, kohlrabi, and onions.

Heat the olive oil and butter in a Dutch oven and brown the meat on all sides on medium heat.

Add the bay leaf, thyme, and clove to the pot. Deglaze with the red wine and reduce slightly.

Peel and quarter the tomatoes, remove the seeds, and coarsely chop the flesh. Add the tomatoes to the meat, pour in some of the stock, and bring to a boil. Cover the pot and stew for at least 2 hours over low heat. Baste the meat from time to time with the stewing liquid, and gradually add the remaining stock.

When the roast has finished cooking, remove it from the pot. Pour the stewing liquid through a fine sieve into a smaller pan, bring to a boil again, and season the sauce to taste with salt and pepper. Slice the roast and place it on a warmed serving platter. Pour the hot sauce over it and sprinkle with the chopped parsley.

Barding

Top round of beef, bacon, and aromatic herbs are needed for a brasato.

Wash the meat, pat it dry, and rub it with salt, pepper, and chopped herbs.

Then cover the meat on all sides with thin slices of fatback or bacon.

To secure the fatback, tie up the meat lengthwise with kitchen twine.

Then wrap the kitchen twine around your hand, loop it around the meat, and pull tight.

Repeat this step until the meat is fully wrapped. Fasten the twine with a knot.

Slowly stew the roast in broth or wine. Let it rest a few minutes before carving.

Remove the twine and cut the meat into uniform slices with a sharp carving knife.

Involtini alla barese
Beef Roulades with Pecorino

8 thin slices of beef, 3½ oz (100 g) each
⅔ cup (80 g) chopped pitted green olives
8 slices coppa ham
3 oz (80 g) medium-aged pecorino cheese, shaved
2 tbsp olive oil
1 onion, finely chopped
1 garlic clove, finely chopped
1 tbsp tomato paste
7 tbsp (100 ml) dry red wine
1 cup (250 ml) beef stock
salt
freshly ground pepper
1 sprig sage

Wash the sliced beef, pat it dry, and pound flat. Finely dice the olives. Lightly season the meat with salt and pepper on both sides and cover each slice with a slice of ham. Sprinkle olives and pecorino on the ham. Roll up the roulades and tie them with kitchen twine.

Heat the olive oil in a pan and brown the roulades on medium heat. Add the onion, garlic, and tomato paste and sauté. Deglaze the pan with the wine, stirring to loosen the pan drippings, and let the liquid reduce.

Pour in the stock, add the sage sprig, place the lid so that it half covers the pan, and braise for 30 to 40 minutes on low heat. Then take the roulades out of the pan, remove the twine, and keep the meat warm. Bring the sauce to a boil and season to taste with salt and pepper. Serve the roulades on warmed plates with sauce poured over them.

Filetto all'alloro
Fillet of Beef in Laurel Wreath

4 beef fillet steaks (tenderloin),
9 oz (250 g) each
4 tsp spicy mustard
12 fresh bay leaves
3 tbsp olive oil
1 tbsp peppercorns, coarsely crushed
¼ cup (60 ml) Italian brandy
salt

Preheat the oven to 265°F (130°C). Brush the edges of the steaks with the mustard. Place 3 bay leaves around each steak and secure with kitchen twine. Season with salt.

Heat the olive oil in an ovenproof pan and thoroughly brown the steaks on both sides, then cook in the oven for 15 to 20 minutes.

Place the steaks on warmed plates. Pour off the frying fat and sprinkle the peppercorns in the pan. Pour in the brandy, heat slightly, then flambé. Drizzle the brandy sauce over the fillets and serve immediately.

Favorite Lamb Dishes

Agnello all'uovo e limone
Lamb Goulash with Egg and Lemon

1¾ lb (800 g) lamb shoulder
2 tbsp flour
1 onion
2 oz (60 g) fatback
2 tbsp oil
1¼ cups (300 ml) white wine
½ cup (125 ml) bouillon
juice of 1 lemon
2 egg yolks
1 garlic clove
salt
freshly ground pepper
grated lemon peel for seasoning

Rinse the lamb, dab it dry, and cut into 1-inch (3-cm) cubes. Salt and pepper the lamb, then sprinkle with the flour. Peel the onion; finely dice it and the fatback.

Heat the oil in a Dutch oven and fry the fatback. Add the lamb in portions and brown it, stirring frequently. Add the onion and fry until translucent. Deglaze with half of the wine, scraping the pan to loosen the pan drippings. Once the wine has reduced, add the bouillon, cover the pot, and simmer for about 1 hour on low heat. Gradually add the rest of the wine.

Remove the pieces of cooked lamb with a slotted spoon and keep warm on a serving plate. Whisk together the lemon juice and egg yolk. Put the garlic through a press and add it to the egg yolk mixture. Bring the pan juices to a boil again and add the egg-lemon mixture, stirring continuously, but do not let the sauce boil. Season the sauce to taste with salt, pepper, and lemon peel. Pour over the lamb and serve hot.

Filetto alle verdure
Fillet of Lamb on Vegetable Pasta

2 carrots
2 small zucchini
3½ oz (100 g) mushrooms
4 lamb fillets, 4–5 oz (130 g) each
2 tbsp clarified butter
1⅔ cups (400 ml) lamb stock
generous ¾ cup (200 g) heavy cream
9 oz (250 g) tagliatelle
4 tbsp butter
salt
freshly ground pepper

Peel the carrots and slice into long strips with a vegetable peeler. Wash the zucchini and also cut lengthwise into thin strips. Bring a pot of lightly salted water to a boil and blanch the vegetable strips for 2 minutes, then refresh them in cold water. Let drain.

Preheat the oven to 210°F (100°C). Clean and thinly slice the mushrooms. Rinse the lamb fillets and pat dry. Salt and pepper the meat. Heat the clarified butter in a pan and brown the fillets on both sides. Place on an ovenproof plate and roast for 20 minutes.

Pour the fat from the pan. Pour in the lamb stock and stir to dissolve the pan drippings in the broth. Add the cream and simmer until the sauce is reduced by half. Bring a large pot of salted water to a boil and cook the tagliatelle until al dente.

Melt the butter in a saucepan and gently sauté the mushrooms. Add the vegetable strips to heat them up. Drain the pasta, then mix with the vegetable strips and mushrooms. Season with salt and pepper.

Remove the meat from the oven and slice it diagonally. Stir the meat juice into the sauce and heat it up. Serve the pasta on warmed plates topped with the meat, with a liberal serving of sauce over it.

Spezzatino di castrato
Mutton Ragout

2¼ lb (1 kg) mutton, shoulder cut
7 tbsp (100 ml) white wine vinegar
2 sprigs rosemary
2–3 garlic cloves
5 tbsp olive oil
14 oz (400 g) canned, peeled tomatoes
2 bay leaves
generous ¾ cup (200 ml) white wine
salt
freshly ground pepper
sugar

Rinse the mutton, pat dry, then remove any skin, tendons, and fat. Cut the meat into bite-size chunks. In a large pot, bring to a boil 4 cups (1 liter) of water, the vinegar, and 1 rosemary sprig. Add the meat cubes to the pot and cook for about 10 minutes, then remove them and drain well.

Chop the garlic and the leaves from the second rosemary sprig. Heat the olive oil in a Dutch oven, add the meat cubes, and brown on all sides. Add the garlic and rosemary and sauté briefly. Season liberally with salt and pepper. Drain the tomatoes and add them to the meat with the bay leaves. Pour on the white wine, then bring everything to a boil. Cover the ragout and stew on low heat for around 1½ hours, stirring occasionally. Remove the lid 15 minutes before the end of cooking time so the sauce can thicken. Adjust the seasoning with salt, pepper, and sugar before serving.

Agnello con olive
Lamb with Black Olives

1¾ lb (800 g) lamb	
2 sprigs rosemary	
1 bay leaf	
½ tsp black peppercorns	
2 garlic cloves	
7 tbsp (100 ml) olive oil	
1 cup (200 g) chickpeas	
1 onion	
1 leek	
2 carrots	
1¼ cup (150 g) black olives	
2 tomatoes	
flour for coating	
4 cups (1 liter) vegetable broth	
1 tsp grated orange rind	
freshly ground pepper	
1 tbsp finely chopped sage	

Cut the meat into bite-size chunks and place it in a bowl. Add the rosemary leaves, bay leaf, peppercorns, and garlic then pour on the olive oil. Cover with plastic wrap and marinate in the refrigerator overnight. Turn the meat several times in the seasoned oil. Soak the chickpeas overnight in plenty of water.

The next day, chop the onion, leek, and carrots into small pieces. Set aside a few olives for garnish; pit and coarsely chop the rest. Peel and quarter the tomatoes, remove the seeds, and cut into fine dice.

Remove the meat from the herbed oil and let drain. Coat it with a little flour, shaking off any excess. Drain the herbed oil through a sieve into a bowl. Pour the water off the chickpeas and drain thoroughly.

Heat 3 tablespoons of the herbed oil in a Dutch oven and lightly brown the meat in it. Add the onion and tomato and cook for a few minutes, then stir in the chickpeas. Pour in the broth and bring to a boil. Cover the pot and simmer for 30 minutes over low heat, then add the olives, leeks, carrots, and orange peel. Stew for another 30 minutes.

Season the lamb ragout with salt and pepper. Serve on warmed plates, sprinkled with sage and garnished with whole olives.

Favorite Pork Dishes

Spezzatino di maiale
Pork Goulash

1¼ lb (600 g) lean pork
2–3 tbsp olive oil
1 tsp fennel seeds
5 garlic cloves, finely chopped
1 fresh red chile, finely chopped
11 oz (300 g) tomatoes, peeled and diced
salt
freshly ground pepper

Wash the meat, pat dry, and cut it into bite-size pieces. Heat the olive oil in a Dutch oven. Add the fennel seeds and garlic to the pot. Season the meat with salt and pepper.

Brown the meat on all sides in the hot olive oil. As soon as the meat browns, add the chile and tomatoes. Cover the pot and stew over low heat for about 1 hour, adding a little warm water as needed.

Polpette dei preti
Priests' Meatloaf

1 pork caul
3½ oz (100 g) prosciutto
3½ oz (100 g) mortadella
soup vegetables, such as carrots, celery, or other root vegetables
1 onion
14 oz (400 g) mixed ground meat
1 egg
3 tbsp breadcrumbs
⅔ cup (75 g) grated Parmesan
1 tbsp clarified butter
4 cups (1 liter) hot milk
1 garlic clove
1 bay leaf
salt
freshly ground pepper

Rinse the pork caul for 30 minutes, then drain. Finely dice the prosciutto and mortadella. Wash and coarsely chop the soup vegetables. Peel and finely dice the onion.

Combine the ground meat with the prosciutto, mortadella, egg, breadcrumbs, and Parmesan. Season with salt and pepper. Form the meat into a loaf. Spread out the drained pork caul, place the meatloaf on it, and wrap with the caul.

Heat the clarified butter in a Dutch oven and briefly brown the meatloaf on all sides. Remove it from the pot, then lightly brown the soup vegetables and onion in the pan drippings. Return the meatloaf to the pot and pour on 1 cup (250 ml) of the hot milk. Mash the garlic clove with a knife and add it to the milk along with the bay leaf. Bring to a boil and simmer, covered, on low heat for about 1 hour. Gradually add the remaining hot milk during that time.

Place the finished meatloaf on a warmed platter. Season the sauce with salt and pepper. Serve the meatloaf with the sauce on the side.

Favorite Chicken and Turkey Dishes

Pollo alla diavola
Spicy Chicken

2 dried red chiles, chopped
2 tbsp lemon juice
3 tbsp orange juice
2 cups (500 ml) white wine
1 bay leaf
1 chicken, ready to cook
salt
freshly ground pepper

In a bowl, stir together the chiles, citrus juices, and wine, then crumble the bay leaf into it.

Cut the neck and wing tips off the chicken. Cut through the chicken along the breastbone and pull it open. Then carefully pound it as flat as possible without damaging the bones in the process. Lay the chicken in a bowl and pour the wine marinade over it. Cover and marinate in the refrigerator for a day, turning it over once.

Remove the chicken from the marinade, pat dry, and rub salt and pepper into it. Grill on a charcoal or gas grill for about 40 minutes until crisp brown, turning periodically.

Pollo alla salvia
Sage Chicken

4 boneless chicken breasts with skin
2 slices prosciutto
8 sage leaves
1 garlic clove
1 tbsp fennel seeds, ground in a mortar
4 tbsp olive oil
½ lime, sliced
salt
freshly ground pepper

Preheat the oven to 340°F (170°C).

Gently loosen the skin on each chicken breast and place half a slice of prosciutto and 1 sage leaf underneath it. Cut the remaining sage leaves into strips. Peel and finely chop the garlic. Season the meat with salt and pepper, then rub the fennel seeds and garlic into it.

Heat the olive oil in a pan. Fry the meat on the skin side first, then on the other side. Remove from the pan and lay in a baking dish. Pour the pan drippings over the chicken, then place the lime slices and remaining sage leaves on top. Cook in the oven for about 30 minutes, then serve on a warmed platter.

Pollo alla Marengo
Marengo Chicken

1 chicken, ready to cook
3 tbsp olive oil
½ cup (125 ml) white wine
2 oz (50 g) pearl onions
2 garlic cloves
2 tbsp flour
2 cups (500 ml) poultry stock
4 small vine tomatoes
7 oz (200 g) small mushrooms
4 crayfish tails, cooked
1 tbsp finely chopped parsley
salt
freshly ground pepper

Wash the chicken, pat dry, and cut it into 4 portions. Rub generous amounts of salt and pepper into the skin. Heat the olive oil in a Dutch oven and brown the chicken quarters on all sides. Deglaze with the white wine, then cover the pot and simmer for 10 minutes.

Peel the pearl onions and garlic. Cut the pearl onions in half and finely chop the garlic. Add both to the chicken, dust with the flour, and cook briefly. Then pour in the poultry stock. Cover the pot and simmer for 20 minutes on medium heat.

Meanwhile, peel the tomatoes and cut into quarters. Cut the mushrooms in half. Add the vegetables to the chicken and season with salt and pepper. If necessary, add a little more wine. Simmer on low heat for another 25 to 30 minutes.

Add the crayfish tails and warm them in the sauce. Sprinkle the parsley over the chicken and serve on warmed plates.

The Battle of Marengo

Marengo, a little village in the Italian province of Alessandria, set the stage for the historic battle of June 14, 1800, in which Napoleon scored a decisive victory over the Austrians. When the glorious commander clamored for something to eat, Dunant, his chef and a native of Switzerland, had to improvise, because he had lost all of his provisions and baggage in the heat of battle. So he sent soldiers off in search of food.

They returned, bringing him chicken, tomatoes, mushrooms, and crayfish, which Dunant ingeniously combined into a very delicious dish, Polla alla Marengo. This fortuitous meal is said to have met with the French emperor's enthusiastic approval, and it has not lost any of its freshness or spontaneity in the past two centuries. Today gourmets in France, Italy, and elsewhere love this uncommon recipe (left).

Pollo alla diavola

Pollo alla cacciatora
Chicken Cacciatore

1 chicken, ready to cook
2 tbsp olive oil
2 oz (50 g) pancetta, diced
1 white onion, finely chopped
½ cup (125 ml) white wine
4 tomatoes
1 cup (250 ml) meat stock
salt
freshly ground pepper

Wash the chicken, pat it dry, and cut it into 8 pieces. Rub generous amounts of salt and pepper into the skin. Heat the olive oil in a Dutch oven and fry the pancetta and onion until the onions are translucent. Add the chicken pieces and brown on all sides. Deglaze the pan with the white wine and simmer for 5 minutes.

Peel and quarter the tomatoes, remove the seeds, and cut into small dice. Add to the chicken, then pour in the meat stock. Cover the pot and stew for 30 to 40 minutes. Season to taste with salt and pepper before serving.

Pollo alla griglia
Grilled Chicken

1 corn-fed chicken,
ca. 2¾ lb (1.2 kg), ready to cook
2 tsp grated lemon rind
3 garlic cloves, thinly sliced
juice of 3 lemons
6 tbsp olive oil
salt
coarsely ground pepper

Wash the chicken, pat it dry, and cut in half lengthwise. Lay the chicken halves in a bowl and season them with pepper. Spread the lemon rind and garlic over the chicken. Pour on the lemon juice and olive oil, then cover and marinate overnight in the refrigerator.

The next day, take the chicken halves out of the marinade and let drain. Season the meat with salt and grill it slowly on a charcoal or gas grill on medium heat until crisp on both sides. Brush the chicken occasionally with the marinade while grilling.

Pollo al vino bianco
Chicken in White Wine

1 chicken, ca. 3 lb (1.3 kg),
ready to cook
2 tbsp olive oil
5–6 oz (150 g) pancetta, diced
5 shallots, diced
1 tbsp flour
3¼ cups (750 ml) white wine
1 sprig rosemary
salt
freshly ground pepper

Wash the chicken, pat it dry, and cut it into portions. Rub each piece with salt and pepper. Preheat the oven to 350°F (175°C).

Heat the olive oil in a roasting pan and brown the meat on all sides. Add the pancetta and shallots and fry. Dust with the flour and pour in the wine. Add the rosemary sprig. Cover the roasting pan and put in the oven for 30 minutes.

After that time, remove the lid from the roasting pan and return the chicken to the oven to continue cooking until the wine has nearly evaporated. Remove the rosemary sprig before serving.

Tacchino ripieno
Turkey with Stuffing

Serves six

1 young turkey, ca. 7–8 lb (3.5 kg),
ready to cook
3½ oz (100 g) pancetta, diced
2 onions, finely chopped
2 tsp dried thyme
2 celery ribs, diced
3 apples, diced
¼ cup (50 g) golden raisins
⅓ cup (50 g) currants
3½ oz (100 g) dried fruits
(apricots, cherries, prunes), diced
2 eggs
¾ cup (75 g) breadcrumbs
2 tbsp olive oil, plus extra for greasing
2 cups (500 ml) poultry stock
½ cup (125 ml) red wine
salt
freshly ground pepper

Wash the turkey and pat it dry. Generously rub with salt and pepper, inside and out. Preheat the oven to 350°F (175°C) and grease a roasting pan with olive oil.

Render the pancetta in a pan. Add the onions and sauté until translucent. Stir in the thyme and celery and sauté for a few minutes. Remove the pan from the stove. Combine the onion mixture with the apples, golden raisins, currants, and dried fruits. Cool slightly, then stir in the eggs and breadcrumbs. Season the stuffing with salt and pepper.

Fill the turkey with the stuffing and close the cavity with wooden skewers. Place the turkey in the roasting pan. Brush the turkey with olive oil. Roast for 3½ to 4 hours, basting from time to time with the poultry stock.

When the turkey is done, remove it from the roasting pan and keep it warm. Pour the pan juices into a pan and skim off the fat. Add the red wine, then boil for several minutes. Season the sauce with salt and pepper and serve with the turkey.

Favorite Vegetable Dishes

Broccoli strascinati
Broccoli with Anchovy Sauce

2¼ lb (1 kg) broccoli
4 anchovy fillets in oil
7 tbsp (100 ml) olive oil
salt
freshly ground pepper

Clean the broccoli and separate it into small florets. Peel the stems, halve or quarter them according to their thickness, and slice thinly.

Bring a pan of salted water to a boil and cook the stems for about 10 minutes, then add the florets and simmer for another 8 to 10 minutes.

Rinse the anchovies in cold, flowing water, then dab them dry and chop finely.

Heat the olive oil in a deep pan. Add the anchovies and mash into a paste. Drain the broccoli well, then combine with the anchovy sauce. Season with pepper and serve hot.

Carote al Marsala
Carrots with Marsala

ca.1 lb (500 g) carrots	
1 white onion	
2 tbsp olive oil	
1 tsp brown sugar	
4 tbsp Marsala	
2 tbsp pine nuts	
salt	
freshly ground pepper	

Peel and thinly slice the carrots. Peel and dice the onion.

Heat the olive oil in a pan and fry the onion. Add the carrots and cook lightly, then sprinkle with the sugar, turn the heat on high, and caramelize the vegetables. Add a scant ¹/₂ cup (100 ml) of water and season with salt and pepper. Over low heat, cook the carrots for an additional 10 minutes, until the water has evaporated. Pour the Marsala over the vegetables and reduce once again.

Heat a pan and dry-roast the pine nuts until golden brown. Before serving, sprinkle them over the carrots.

Cavolo in umido
Stewed Savoy Cabbage

1 small savoy cabbage	
2 tbsp olive oil	
1 tbsp butter	
1 small onion, finely chopped	
juice of 1 lemon	
1 cup (250 ml) vegetable broth	
2 bay leaves	
1/8 tsp ground allspice	
salt	
freshly ground pepper	
freshly grated nutmeg	

Clean the cabbage, cut it in quarters, and remove the stalk with a wedge-shaped cut so that the leaves remain attached.

Heat the olive oil and butter in a large pot and sauté the onion. Add the cabbage quarters and briefly fry. Sprinkle with the lemon juice and pour the broth over the cabbage. Add the bay leaves and season with the allspice, salt, pepper, and nutmeg. Cover the pot and stew the cabbage on medium heat for 25 to 30 minutes.

For the sauce, first peel the tomatoes, remove the seeds, and cut into cubes.

Sauté the onion, garlic, and tomatoes in olive oil, then add the wine.

Involtini di cavolo verza
Stuffed Cabbage

1¾ lb (750 g) plum tomatoes	
¼ cup (60 ml) olive oil	
1 white onion, finely chopped	
2 garlic cloves, finely chopped	
½ cup (125 ml) white wine	
1 pinch sugar	
8 large savoy cabbage leaves	
7 oz (200 g) buffalo mozzarella	
1½ cups (200 g) cooked rice	
1 egg	
2 tbsp finely chopped parsley	
salt	
freshly ground pepper	

Briefly blanch the savoy cabbage leaves in lightly salted water.

Remove the thick rib in the center with a wedge-shaped cut.

Peel and quarter the tomatoes, remove the seeds, and cut into dice. Heat 3 tablespoons of the olive oil in a pot and sauté the onion and garlic. Add the tomatoes and wine, then season with the sugar and salt and pepper. Simmer on low heat for 20 minutes.

Bring a large pot of salted water to a boil and briefly blanch the cabbage leaves. Remove them with a slotted spoon and refresh in cold water. Place them in a strainer to drain.

For the filling, finely dice the mozzarella and mix it with the rice, egg, and parsley. Season to taste with salt and pepper.

Place the cabbage leaves on a work surface and place a spoonful of filling in the middle of each leaf. Fold over the edges, starting at the bottom, and roll into a bundle. If necessary, tie with kitchen string.

Heat the remaining olive oil in a pan and briefly fry the roulades on both sides. Lay the roulades in the tomato sauce with the seams facing down. Cover the pan and stew for about 40 minutes on low heat. If the sauce becomes too thick, add a little water or wine as needed.

Place a portion of the rice-mozzarella filling on the center of each leaf.

Then fold the top part of the leaf over the filling.

Next, fold the sides of the cabbage leaf over the filling and roll it up.

Fry the roulades in olive oil and lay them in the tomato sauce.

Fish, Meat & Vegetables 73

Favorite Vegetable Dishes from the Oven

Finocchi gratinati
Fennel Gratin

4 fennel bulbs
1 tbsp lemon juice
2 tbsp butter, plus extra for greasing
2 tbsp flour
2 cups (500 ml) warm milk
7 tbsp (100 ml) heavy cream
2 tbsp white wine
generous 1 cup (25 g) grated fontina cheese
generous ¼ cup (50 g) pine nuts
salt
freshly ground pepper
freshly grated nutmeg

Remove the fennel greens and set aside. Slice the bulbs about ¼ inch (5 mm) thick and blanch in boiling salted water, with the lemon juice, for 3 minutes. Remove the fennel with a slotted spoon and refresh in cold water, then drain. Preheat the oven to 350°F (175°C) and grease a baking dish with butter.

In a heavy pot, melt the butter, stir in the flour, and cook briefly. While stirring continuously, add the warm milk and cream and let the sauce thicken. Blend in the white wine and season to taste with salt, pepper, and nutmeg.

Lay the fennel slices in the baking dish. Pour the sauce over the fennel and sprinkle the cheese on top, then bake for about 25 minutes, or until golden brown.

Heat a pan and dry-roast the pine nuts until golden brown. Finely chop the fennel greens. Before serving, sprinkle the greens and roasted pine nuts over the gratin.

Peperoni ripieni
Stuffed Bell Peppers

2 red bell peppers
2 yellow bell peppers
7 anchovy fillets in oil
4 tomatoes
⅓ cup (75 ml) olive oil, plus extra for greasing
1 white onion, finely chopped
2 tbsp finely chopped parsley
2 tbsp grated Parmesan
2 tbsp breadcrumbs
salt
freshly ground pepper

Wash the bell peppers, halve them lengthwise, and remove the cores. Rinse the anchovies under cold water, dab dry, then chop them finely. Peel and quarter the tomatoes, remove the seeds, and cut into dice. Preheat the oven to 450°F (230°C) and grease a baking dish with olive oil.

Heat 2 tablespoons of the olive oil and fry the anchovies and onion. Tip them into a bowl and mix with the tomatoes, parsley, Parmesan, and breadcrumbs. Season the mixture with salt and pepper, then fill the bell pepper halves with it.

Place the stuffed bell peppers side by side in the baking dish. Cover it with aluminum foil and bake for 15 minutes. Remove the foil, sprinkle peppers with the remaining olive oil, and bake another 10 to 15 minutes. Serve hot or cold.

Cavolini di Bruxelles alla panna
Scalloped Brussels Sprouts

2¼ lb (1 kg) Brussels sprouts
4 tbsp butter, plus extra for greasing
1 onion, finely chopped
1 garlic clove, finely chopped
1 cup (250 ml) vegetable broth
2 eggs
1 cup (250 ml) heavy cream
generous ½ cup (60 g) grated Parmesan
salt
freshly ground pepper
freshly grated nutmeg

Preheat the oven to 350°F (175°C) and grease a baking dish with butter. Trim the Brussels sprouts. Melt half the butter in a saucepan and sauté the onions and garlic until the onions are translucent. Add the Brussels sprouts, season with salt, pepper, and nutmeg, and pour on the broth. Cover the pan and simmer on medium heat for 15 minutes.

Pour the Brussels sprouts and cooking liquid into the baking dish. Whisk the eggs and cream together and pour over the Brussels sprouts. Sprinkle with the Parmesan and dot with the remaining butter. Bake for about 20 minutes.

Wash the beets, dab dry and wrap individually in aluminum foil.

After baking, unwrap the beets and let them cool slightly.

Barbabietole al forno
Baked Red Beets
with Balsamic Vinaigrette

generous 1 lb (500 g) red beets
2 tbsp balsamic vinegar
1 tsp mustard
5 tbsp olive oil
salt and pepper
1 small handful fresh mint

Preheat the oven to 390°F (200°C). Wash and dry the beets and wrap each one individually in aluminum foil. Place them on a baking sheet and bake 40 to 60 minutes, depending on their size.

When cooked, remove the beets from the foil, let them cool, then peel. Beets stain skin dramatically, so kitchen gloves are recommended. Slice the beets and arrange them on a serving platter.

Whisk together the vinegar, mustard, and olive oil, season with salt and pepper, and pour the dressing over the beets. Wash the mint, dab dry, and pluck the leaves. Cut them into narrow strips and sprinkle over the beets.

Potatoes

In Italy, potatoes are not merely a filling side dish, but—like all other vegetables—are significant in their own right. The nutritious tubers are fried with aromatic herbs, or used as the main ingredient in casseroles and vegetable timbales. Especially in northern Italy, potatoes also make their way to the table in the form of gnocchi.

Spanish conquistadors "discovered" the potato in the Andes in the sixteenth century. The Incas prepared dishes out of these tubers that greatly appealed to the Spaniards. Since at first sight the invaders thought that these new vegetables growing underground were truffles, they called the unknown food Incan *taratoufli*.

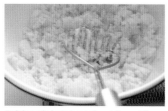

Peel the cooked potatoes and mash them while they are still warm.

Thoroughly wash the spinach, removing any wilted leaves or coarse stems.

Purée the parsley and spinach with a handheld mixer until smooth.

Stir the spinach purée, eggs, and cream into the mashed potatoes.

Fill a round baking dish with the potato-spinach mixture and bake.

Timballo verde
Vegetable Timbale

1¼ lb (600 g) mealy potatoes
generous 1 lb (500 g) leaf spinach
1 tbsp olive oil
1 white onion, finely chopped
2 bunches parsley
4 eggs
7 tbsp (100 ml) heavy cream
scant 1 cup (100 g) grated Parmesan
3 tbsp butter, plus extra for greasing
salt
freshly ground pepper
freshly grated nutmeg

Bring a large pot of salted water to a boil. Wash the potatoes and cook them, in their skins, for about 20 minutes.

Thoroughly wash the spinach, removing any wilted leaves and coarse stems. Heat the olive oil in a pan and briefly sauté the onion, then add the dripping-wet spinach. Cover the pan and steam for 2 to 3 minutes. Pour off the water and let the spinach drain. Peel and mash the potatoes while still hot.

Preheat the oven to 350°F (175°C) and grease a round baking dish with butter. Wash the parsley, dab it dry, and pluck the leaves. Purée the parsley and spinach with a handheld mixer. Season with salt, pepper, and nutmeg.

Whisk the eggs and cream together and stir into the mashed potatoes. Stir in the spinach purée and half the Parmesan, and season again with salt and pepper.

Fill the baking dish with the potato-spinach mixture. Sprinkle the remaining Parmesan and dot the butter on top. Bake for about 25 minutes, or until golden brown.

Patate al rosmarino
Rosemary Potatoes

1¾ lb (750 g) waxy potatoes
3 garlic cloves
3 sprigs rosemary
⅓ cup (75 ml) olive oil, plus extra for greasing
salt
freshly ground pepper

Wash and peel the potatoes and cut them into small cubes. Peel and coarsely chop the garlic. Pluck the leaves from the rosemary and coarsely chop them, as well. Preheat the oven to 390°F (200°C). Grease a flat baking dish with olive oil.

Place a layer of potatoes on the bottom of the baking dish. Season with some of the garlic and rosemary, salt, and pepper. Repeat this procedure until all the ingredients have been used. Drizzle the olive oil over the top and bake for about 45 minutes, tossing the potatoes several times. Serve in the baking dish while hot.

Favorite
Egg Dishes

Frittata con prezzemolo
Frittata with Parsley

1 bunch flat-leaf parsley
6 eggs
4 tbsp olive oil
salt
freshly ground pepper

Rinse and dab dry the parsley, then coarsely chop the leaves. Beat the eggs in a bowl with some salt and pepper until foamy, then blend in the parsley.

Heat the olive oil in a heavy pan until it starts to smoke. Pour in the eggs and smooth the surface with a wooden spatula. Reduce the heat to low and let the eggs thicken.

As soon as the frittata begins to brown on the underside, use a lid or plate to carefully turn over the omelet. Cook the other side until it is golden brown. Cut the frittata into 4 slices and serve while hot or warm.

The classic frittata is prepared with fresh eggs, parsley, salt, and pepper.

Beat the eggs with salt and pepper until they are foamy, and then stir in parsley.

Heat olive oil in a pan and pour in the eggs.

Fry the omelet on both sides until golden brown.

Frittata di carciofi
Artichoke Frittata

6 artichoke hearts in oil
1 handful arugula
6 eggs
3 tbsp heavy cream
1 tbsp finely chopped parsley
2 tbsp olive oil
1 tbsp butter
1 onion, finely diced
1 garlic clove, finely diced
salt
freshly ground pepper

Drain and quarter the artichoke hearts. Thoroughly wash the arugula, removing any wilting leaves and coarse stems, and chop the leaves.

Whisk the eggs and cream together, then season with salt and pepper and stir in the chopped parsley.

Heat the olive oil and butter in a nonstick pan. Fry the onion and garlic until the onion is translucent. Add the artichokes and cook briefly. Pour the egg-cream mixture over the artichokes and reduce the heat. As soon as the surface solidifies, use a lid or plate to gently turn the frittata over and cook the other side until golden brown.

Serve the frittata hot, or let it cool and cut it into bite-size pieces.

Crespelle Basic Recipe

3 eggs
1¼ cups (150 g) flour
1 cup (250 ml) milk
1 pinch salt
¼ cup (60 g) butter

Beat the eggs, then stir in the flour and milk to make a thin batter. Season with a pinch of salt. Let the batter rest for 30 minutes.

Melt a little butter in a nonstick pan and pour in one small ladle of batter. Swivel the pan to distribute the batter evenly. Fry the *crespelle* on both sides until golden brown, then set aside and keep warm.

Repeat this procedure to make 8 *crespelle*.

Crespelle al prosciutto di Parma
Crespelle with Prosciutto

8 crespelle (see basic recipe)
3 tbsp olive oil, plus extra for greasing
1 small onion, finely chopped
1 garlic clove, finely chopped
14 oz (400 g) canned diced tomatoes
1 tbsp chopped basil
3½ oz (100 g) prosciutto, thinly sliced
½ cup (50 g) grated Parmesan
salt
freshly ground pepper

Prepare the crespelle according to the basic recipe and let them cool slightly. Heat 2 tablespoons of the olive oil and sauté the onion and garlic until the onion is translucent, then add the tomatoes. Season with the basil, salt, and pepper and simmer for 10 minutes. Preheat the oven to 435°F (225°C) and grease a baking dish with olive oil.

Lay the prosciutto slices on the crespelle, roll them up, and arrange side by side in the baking dish. Cover with the tomato sauce and sprinkle with the Parmesan and remaining olive oil. Bake for about 15 minutes.

Crespelle al forno
Crespelle Gratin

8 crespelle (see basic recipe)
11 oz (300 g) assorted wild mushrooms
3½ tbsp (50 g) butter
1 small onion, finely chopped
3½ oz (100 g) cooked ham,
cut into strips
2 tbsp chopped parsley
2 cups (500 ml) béchamel sauce
3½ oz (100 g) Gorgonzola, crumbled
salt
freshly ground pepper

Prepare the crespelle according to the basic recipe and let them cool slightly. Wash the mushrooms and cut into thin slices. Preheat the oven to 435°F (225°C) and grease a baking dish with 1½ tablespoons of the butter.

Heat the remaining butter and sauté the onion until translucent, then add the ham and mushrooms. Stirring constantly, sauté for about 10 minutes, until the liquid has thickened. Stir in the parsley and remove the pan from the stovetop.

Season the mushrooms with salt and pepper and place some on each crespelle. Roll them up and arrange side by side in the baking dish. Pour the béchamel sauce over the crespelle and sprinkle with crumbled Gorgonzola. Bake for about 15 minutes.

DESSERTS

Favorite Desserts

The palette of Italian desserts is as colorful and multifaceted as the land itself. One could simplify by distinguishing different categories of *dolci*: fruit desserts, creamy desserts and puddings (which are most often turned out of molds), and frozen or semifrozen treats. The scale of the recipes ranges from simple to complicated, from unostentatious to elegant—although complicated methods of preparation are no guarantee of a delicious dessert. As in all other areas of the culinary arts, the optimal quality of the products used is of primary importance. Fruits should have reached their full flavor, that is, they should be ripe but not overripe. Mousses should always be given enough time to chill, thereby allowing them to firm in the mold.

Most desserts are portioned and served on plates, decorated with herbs, nuts, cream, confectioners' sugar, or cocoa. If more than one dessert is served on a single plate, it is important that the flavors harmonize rather than overshadow one another. Neutral accompaniments include a fruit coulis, ladyfingers, or ice cream, preferably homemade. Always valid is the dictum that a few good ingredients are often worth more than an abundance of unmanageable flavors.

Pere al vino rosso
Pears in Red Wine

3¼ cups (750 ml) full-bodied red wine
1 cup + 2 tbsp (250 g) sugar
1 cinnamon stick
2 cloves
2¼ lb (1 kg) small, firm pears

Preheat the oven to 300°F (150°C). Combine the wine and sugar in a saucepan, add the cinnamon stick and cloves, and bring to a boil.

Place the unpeeled pears, with stems facing upward, in a deep baking dish. Pour the hot, spiced wine over the pears and bake for 1 hour, or until soft but not falling apart. Remove from the oven and let the pears cool in the wine. Slice and serve warm or cold. Cooking time may vary according to type of pear, so test them often.

Fragole all'aceto balsamico
Strawberries with
Balsamic Vinegar

generous 1 lb (500 g) strawberries
2 tbsp superfine sugar
2–3 tbsp high-quality balsamic vinegar
several mint leaves to decorate

Remove the stems from the strawberries and cut them in half or quarter, according to size. Sprinkle the sugar, then the vinegar over the berries and mix carefully. Cover with plastic wrap and let rest for at least 1 hour. Before serving, gently mix again and garnish with mint leaves.

Pesche ripiene
Stuffed Peaches

4 firm yellow peaches
1 tbsp lemon juice
3 oz (75 g) candied lemon peel
¾ cup (75 g) crumbled amaretti
3 tbsp sugar
1 egg yolk
2½ tbsp (50 ml) Marsala
8 blanched almonds
1 cup (250 ml) white wine
butter for greasing

Preheat the oven to 350°F (175°C) and grease a baking dish with butter.

Cut the peaches in half and carefully twist the halves apart, removing the pits. Sprinkle with the lemon juice.

Finely chop the candied lemon peel. Combine it with the amaretti, sugar, egg yolk, and Marsala. Fill the peach halves with the mixture and press one almond into the center of each. Place the peach halves next to each other in the baking dish and pour on the white wine. Bake for 15 to 20 minutes. Serve warm or cold in the wine sauce.

Almonds

Native to the Middle East, the almond tree grows throughout the Mediterranean basin. In antiquity, its aromatic and slightly sweet seeds were already prized not only as a healthy food, but also for their medicinal properties. Almonds contain many valuable fatty acids, vitamins, and minerals. In Italy, they are a popular ingredient for a wide range of confections, cakes, and other baked goods.

Sugared almonds are traditionally associated with Italian weddings; newlyweds send little packages containing five sugar-covered almonds as a token of thanks for the gifts they receive. The nuts symbolize health, prosperity, fruitfulness, happiness, and long life. Sugared almonds from Sulmona in Abruzzo are especially famous. Approximately 500 tons of their sugared almonds are sent throughout the world every year.

Pesche ripiene

Mele cotte al vino bianco
Apples in White Wine

2¼ lb (1 kg) apples	
5 tbsp lemon juice	
2 cups (250 ml) white wine	
1 cup (200 g) sugar	
1 cinnamon stick	
2 cloves	

Peel, quarter, and core the apples. Cut them into narrow wedges and immediately sprinkle with the lemon juice.

Combine the wine, sugar, cinnamon stick, and cloves in a saucepan and slowly bring to a boil. Add the apples and simmer on low heat for 10 minutes. Remove the apples with a slotted spoon and set them aside.

Bring the wine to a boil again and reduce to a thick syrup. Remove the cinnamon stick and cloves. Return the apple wedges to the pan and let them cool in the sauce.

Bianco mangiare
Blancmange

3 sheets leaf gelatin
or 1 envelope clear gelatin (¼ oz)

---

1 cup (250 ml) milk

---

generous ¾ cup (100 g) ground almonds

⅓ cup (75 g) sugar

---

2 tsp vanilla sugar

---

1 tsp almond extract

---

1 cup (250 ml) heavy cream

Soak the gelatin in cold water. Combine the milk, almonds, and sugar in a saucepan and slowly bring to a boil. Drain or press the liquid from the gelatin. Remove the hot milk from the stovetop and dissolve the gelatin in it, then stir in the vanilla sugar and almond extract. Pour through a sieve into a bowl and let cool.

As soon as the mixture starts to become firm, whip the cream and fold it in. Rinse 4 small soufflé dishes with cold water and fill. Cover and chill in the refrigerator for at least 3 hours. Before serving, dip dishes briefly into hot water, then turn over onto plates.

Crema di marroni
Sweet Chestnut Mousse

generous 1 lb (500 g) sweet chestnuts

3½ tbsp (50 g) sugar

---

2 tsp vanilla sugar

---

1 pinch cinnamon

---

generous ¾ cup (200 ml) heavy cream

---

salt

---

amaretti to garnish

Preheat the oven to 390°F (200°C). Cut an X into the rounded side of each chestnut, then lay with their flat side on a baking sheet and roast for about 20 minutes, until the shells open. Peel the chestnuts and remove the brown membrane.

Put the chestnuts in a pan. Add just enough water to barely cover them and a little salt. Simmer on low heat for about 40 minutes. Drain the chestnuts, then purée them in a food processor. Mix in the sugar, vanilla sugar, and cinnamon and let cool.

Whip the cream and fold it into the cooled chestnut purée. Portion into dessert bowls and garnish with amaretti.

Sweet Chestnuts

There are two types of edible chestnuts: marrons, or *marroni*, and sweet chestnuts, or *castagne*. The true marron is only found in Italy, the Swiss canton of Tessin, and certain regions of France and Spain. Their fruit is somewhat flatter than the common chestnut and is easier to shell. Because of this—and because their flavor is creamier and more intense than that of the common chestnut—they are preferred in the kitchen. At Italian markets, marrons are sold in fall, fresh from the trees and still in the shell. In grocery stores, one can buy them in cans or jars, already shelled and cooked or puréed.

For centuries, marrons were considered a satisfying staple food—a poor man's potato. Italians said it grew on the *albero del pane*, or "bread tree." Due to the chestnut's high starch content, the nuts were ground into flour and used in bread baking. Today, flat loaves of chestnut bread—traditionally baked on hot stones—are sold in Italy as regional specialties. Candied or glazed chestnuts are enjoyed throughout the country as a delicacy.

Cinnamon

Cinnamon is produced from the bark of thin branches of the evergreen cinnamon tree. The bark is freed of its outer mantel of cork, dried, and then cut into pieces. Cinnamon is one of the oldest spices in the world and has its origins in Ceylon, today's Sri Lanka. As has always been the case, the best cinnamon still comes from this island. It is sold as true Ceylon cinnamon, or canela, in sticks or as powder and lends not only desserts, but also meat and vegetable dishes, a distinctive aroma.

Frutti di bosco con gelato
Forest Berries
with Vanilla Ice Cream

2¼ cups (250 g) fresh red currants
1¾ cups (250 g) fresh blackberries
1¾ cups (250 g) fresh blueberries
2 tbsp confectioners' sugar
juice of ½ lemon
juice of 1 orange
¼ cup (60 ml) amaretto
8 slices or scoops vanilla ice cream
fresh mint leaves to decorate

Sort the berries and place them in a bowl. Combine the confectioners' sugar with the lemon and orange juices and amaretto, then pour over the berries. Mix carefully and let stand for 15 minutes.

Place the slices or scoops of ice cream on 4 plates, then top with the berry mixture. Decorate with mint leaves.

Creme caramel
Crème Caramel

1 cup + 2 tbsp (250 g) sugar
1 vanilla bean
1¼ cups (300 ml) heavy cream
1¼ cups (300 ml) milk
4 eggs
2 egg yolks

In a small saucepan, heat ⅔ cup (150 g) of sugar and 5 tablespoons of water until the sugar caramelizes. Pour the hot caramel into 4 small soufflé dishes and let cool. Preheat the oven to 300°F (150°C).

Cut the vanilla bean lengthwise and scrape out the seeds. Combine the cream and milk in a pan, add the vanilla bean and seeds, and slowly bring to a boil. Remove from the stovetop and take out the vanilla bean.

Beat the eggs and egg yolks with the remaining sugar. Stir in the warm vanilla milk, then pour into the soufflé dishes. Set the soufflés in a baking dish and add enough boiling water in the bottom so that the soufflé dishes are two-thirds submerged. Place the water bath in the oven for about 40 minutes. Remove the soufflé dishes from the water bath, let cool, and chill in the refrigerator overnight to firm.

Before serving, dip the bottom of each soufflé dish briefly into hot water, then turn over onto dessert plates.

Granita di cachi
Persimmon Granita with Chile

generous ¾ cup (100 g) unsalted pistachios
4 persimmons
1 fresh chile
½ cup (100 g) sugar
7 tbsp (100 ml) water
juice and grated peel of 1 lemon

Dry-roast the pistachios in a pan without any added fat, then chop them and set aside.

Wash the persimmons, dab dry, and remove the stems. Cut them into small pieces. Halve the chile lengthwise, remove the seeds, and chop finely. Bring the sugar and water to a boil in a small pan and cook until the syrup is slightly thickened. Cool slightly, then stir in the lemon juice, lemon peel, and chile.

Purée the fruit and syrup in a food processor. Stir in half the pistachios, then transfer to a metal bowl and place in the freezer. When the mixture begins to harden, use a whisk to stir the fruit frozen to the side of the bowl toward the center. Continue to freeze in this manner until it has a creamy texture. When completely frozen, set the bowl in the refrigerator for 30 minutes to thaw slightly.

Serve portions in champagne glasses with the remaining pistachios sprinkled on top.

Sorbetto sprizzetto
Sparkling Sorbet

2 cups (500 ml) white wine
peel of 1 lemon
generous ¾ cup (175 g) sugar
juice of 1 orange
7 tbsp (100 ml) Aperol
¾ cup (200 ml) Prosecco
fresh mint leaves to decorate

Combine the wine, lemon peel, and sugar in a saucepan and slowly bring to a boil. Simmer 1 to 2 minutes, remove from the stovetop, stir in the orange juice, and let cool.

Pour the wine syrup through a fine sieve into a bowl and blend in the Aperol liqueur. Pour the mixtue into an ice cream machine and process to sorbet.

Serve the sorbet in long-stemmed cocktail glasses, pour on the Prosecco, and garnish with mint leaves.

The Classics

Three famous desserts represent Italian cuisine throughout the world: *tiramisù, panna cotta,* and *zabaione.* Their international reputation is well established—for many gourmets, without any one of these sinfully creamy delights, a Mediterranean menu is simply incomplete.

Tiramisù (literally, "pull me up") most likely derives its name from the fact that this perfect mix of espresso, cocoa, sugar, and liqueur has an invigorating effect. The original recipe probably has its roots in Tuscany. This dessert's first incarnation was reputedly created in Siena toward the end of the seventeenth century to honor Grand Duke Cosimo III de' Medici. For this famous connoisseur, the confectioners selected only the finest ingredients, such as mascarpone made from pure buffalo milk, and perfected their creation with the luxury items chocolate and coffee. The result greatly pleased the grand duke and his female coterie. *Tiramisù* immediately earned a reputation for being not only rich, but also stimulating in every respect.

Panna cotta (literally, "baked cream") hails from the region of Emilia-Romagna.

This molded custard numbers among the most delicate temptations northern Italy has to offer, where it is always served with a sauce made of fresh fruit, caramel, or chocolate. In other regions, it is also served with marinated fruit.

Zabaione, a light, foamy cream originally made with dry white wine, is a traditional specialty of the Piedmont region. There it is served not only as a dessert, but there is also an unsweetened version that accompanies cooked mixed vegetables. The name of this delicate wine mousse supposedly derives from San Giovanni di Baylon, the patron saint of bakers. The name of its inventor remains just as mysterious as its age. Whereas some sources honor Bartolomeo Scappi, an Italian cook who lived in the sixteenth century, with this distinction, others claim that it made its first appearance in the eighteenth century at the court of Duke Charles Emmanuel of Savoy.

Ingredients of tiramisù are eggs, mascarpone, ladyfingers, grated chocolate, sugar, and espresso. Tiramisù can be prepared in a rectangular form (as described in the recipe) or dome-shaped (as shown in the photo below).

Tiramisù

3 egg yolks	
4 tbsp amaretto	
¾ cup (150 g) superfine sugar	
2 oz (50 g) bittersweet chocolate, finely grated	
2¼ cups (500 g) mascarpone	
generous ¾ cup (200 ml) heavy cream	
24 ladyfingers	
2 cups (500 ml) strong espresso	
cocoa powder for dusting	

Whisk together the egg yolks and amaretto. Gradually add the sugar and beat until the sugar has dissolved completely. Stir in the chocolate and mascarpone. Whip the cream and fold it in.

Dip the unsugared side of each ladyfinger into the espresso. Arrange half of the ladyfingers on the bottom of a square or rectangular dish, then cover with half of the mascarpone cream. Layer the remaining ladyfingers and cream, spreading it evenly.

Cover the dish and chill overnight in the refrigerator. Before serving, dust heavily with cocoa powder.

Fold the mascarpone and whipped cream into the mixture of eggs, sugar, and grated chocolate.

Stir amaretto into the resulting cream and put half of it into a pastry bag.

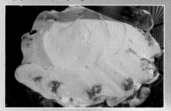

Arrange the ladyfingers on a round serving plate and squeeze some of the cream on top.

Spread the cream evenly. Repeat in several layers and finish with decorative mounds of cream.

Chill the dessert overnight. Before serving, dust heavily with cocoa powder.

Zabaione

4 egg yolks
4 tbsp sugar
½ cup (125 ml) Marsala
1 tsp grated lemon peel

Use a whisk to beat the egg yolks, sugar, and 1 tablespoon of warm water in a metal bowl until they are thick and very pale.

Place the bowl in a hot water bath and continue to whisk, gradually adding the Marsala. Whisk until the mixture is thick and foamy. Remove the bowl from the water bath, add the lemon peel, and continue to beat until the Zabaione is lukewarm. Pour into dessert bowls and serve immediately. Zabaione can be served with amaretti or ladyfingers, or poured over fresh berries.

For zabaione, whisk the egg yolks with the sugar into a thick, pale cream.

Beat the mixture in a hot water bath until foamy, gradually adding the Marsala.

Panna Cotta

1 vanilla bean
2 cups (500 ml) heavy cream
4½ tbsp (60 g) sugar
4 sheets or 1½ envelopes clear gelatin
generous 1 lb (500 g) strawberries
3 tbsp confectioners' sugar

Cut the vanilla bean lengthwise and scrape out the seeds. In a pan, bring the cream to a boil with the vanilla bean and seeds. Stir in the sugar. Simmer on low heat for 15 minutes.

Soak the gelatin in cold water for about 10 minutes, then drain or press the liquid from the gelatin. Pour the hot cream through a strainer into a bowl, then dissolve the gelatin in it. Rinse 4 small soufflé dishes in cold water and fill with the cream. Chill overnight in the refrigerator.

Clean the strawberries, setting aside a few for decoration. Cook the remaining strawberries with the confectioners' sugar. While hot, press the berries through a strainer into a bowl and then let cool.

To serve, unmold the soufflé dishes onto dessert plates, top with strawberry sauce, and decorate with the reserved whole berries.

Favorite Cakes and Pies

Crostata di limone
Lemon Pie

1½ cups (200 g) flour
1 cup + 2 tbsp (250 g) sugar
5 egg yolks
grated peel and juice of 2 lemons
1 pinch salt
7 tbsp (100 g) chilled butter
3 eggs
⅔ cup (150 ml) heavy cream
2 tbsp confectioners' sugar
oil for greasing

Sift the flour onto a work surface, blend in 7 tablespoons (100 g) of sugar, and make a well in the center. Add 4 egg yolks, half the lemon peel, the salt, and the butter, cut into small pieces. Knead everything into a smooth, supple dough. Form the dough into a ball, cover it in plastic wrap, and chill for 1 hour in the refrigerator.

Preheat the oven to 350°F (175°C) and grease a 10-inch (26-cm) springform pan.

On a floured surface, roll out the dough very thin and line the bottom and sides of the pan with it. Use a fork to prick several holes in the dough, then lay a sheet of parchment paper over it. Fill the crust with dried beans to prevent buckling and bake for 15 minutes. Remove the dried beans and parchment paper and let the crust cool.

Preheat the oven to 320°F (160°C). Beat the remaining egg yolk, the whole eggs, and the rest of the sugar and lemon peel into a thick, pale cream. Stir in the lemon juice. Whip the cream and fold it into the egg mixture. Spoon it into the crust and spread it evenly, then bake for 20 minutes. Dust the surface with confectioners' sugar, then return to the oven until golden brown.

Torta di zucca
Pumpkin Cake

1¼ cups (175 g) flour
8½ tbsp (125 g) butter, plus extra for greasing
1 cup (200 g) sugar
1 pinch salt
1 cup (250 ml) milk
½ cup (125 g) short-grain rice
18 oz (500 g) pumpkin flesh
2 eggs, whisked
½ cup (100 g) ricotta
2 tsp vanilla sugar
2 tbsp breadcrumbs
freshly ground pepper

Sift the flour onto a work surface and make a well in the center. Add 5 tablespoons of butter cut in small pieces, half of the sugar, the salt, and ⅓ cup (75–85 ml) of water and knead everything into a smooth, supple dough. Form the dough into ball, cover it in plastic wrap, and chill for 1 hour in the refrigerator.

Combine the milk, 1 cup (250 ml) of water, and the rice in a pan and bring to a boil. Boil for 2 minutes, then remove from the stove and set aside, covered, to cool.

Melt the remaining butter in a pan. Cut the pumpkin flesh into small cubes and cook in the butter until the liquid is absorbed. Purée the pumpkin and stir it into the rice. Stir in the eggs, ricotta, remaining sugar, vanilla sugar, and a little pepper.

Preheat the oven to 390°F (200°C). Grease a 9½-inch (24-cm) springform pan and coat the inside with the breadcrumbs.

Roll out the dough on a floured surface and line the bottom and sides of the pan with it. Use a fork to prick several holes in the dough. Spread the rice and pumpkin mixture evenly in the pan and bake 35 to 40 minutes.

Crostata di limone

Crostata di visciole
Cherry Pie

2¼ cups (500 g) flour
⅔ cup (150 g) superfine sugar
1 pinch salt
2 eggs
grated peel of 1 orange
⅓ cup (75 g) cold butter
⅓ cup (75 g) fresh lard
14 oz (400 g) sour cherry jam
1 egg yolk, whisked
2 tbsp confectioners' sugar
oil for greasing

Sift the flour onto a work surface, blend in the sugar, and make a well in the center. Add the salt, eggs, orange peel, butter, and lard and knead everything into a smooth, supple dough. Form the dough into ball, cover it in plastic wrap, and chill for 1 hour in the refrigerator.

Preheat the oven to 350°F (175°C) and grease an 11-inch (28-cm) springform pan.

On a floured surface, roll out two-thirds of the dough very thin and line the bottom and sides of the pan with it. Spread the jam evenly over the dough.

Roll out the remaining dough and use a pastry wheel to cut it into strips about ¾ inch (2 cm) wide. Use the strips to form a lattice over the jam. Brush the top of the pie with the whisked egg yolk, then bake for about 45 minutes.

Let the pie cool briefly in the springform, then transfer it to a cooling rack. Before serving, dust with confectioners' sugar.

Picture credits

The publisher would like to thank the following for permission to reproduce copyright material.
All product photographs and cutouts: Martin Kurtenbach, Jürgen Schulzki, Ruprecht Stempell. All other photographs Martin Kurtenbach.

Except the following:
Gunter Beer: all wood backgrounds; 8 (top right & bottom left); 10 (top left & top centre); 11; 12, 13 (except cutout); 16 (steps & large); 17; 18; 20-21(large); 22; 26; 27; 28; 29; 30; 31; 32; 33; 36 (top left); 37; 40; 44; 45; 46; 47; 49; 51; 55; 56; 57; 60; 61; 63; 64; 65; 67; 68; 70; 71; 72; 73; 74; 75; 76; 77; 79 (top right); 83; 84; 86; 87; 88; 89; 94; 95

2 Sandra Ivany/Brand X; 6 Atlantide Phototravel; 8 Botanik Bildarchiv Laux (bottom right); 10 Ruprecht Stempell (top left); 14 Sandro Vannini (top); 15 Sandro Vannini (top); Ruprecht Stempell (steps); 25 Jean-Bernard Vernier (box); 34 Poisson d'Avril/photocuisine; 42 Y. Bagros/photocuisine (top right); Jürgen Schulzki (top right); Sandra Ivany/Brand X (bottom right); 58-59 Jürgen Schulzki; 69 Ruprecht Stempell (top left); 80 Gunter Beer (top left & bottom right)

Contents page: Jürgen Schulzki (beef); Gunter Beer (scampi); Grand Tour (Verona); Gunter Beer (dessert); Grand Tour (Lake Como); Mark Bolton (Venice); Sergio Pitamitz (Tuscany)

96